Teacher's Guide

COME, FOLLOW ME
(Revised Edition)

A Study Book For Acolytes

Edwin B. Womack

CSS Publishing Company, Inc., Lima, Ohio

COME, FOLLOW ME (REVISED EDITION)
TEACHER'S GUIDE

Scripture quotations marked (NRSV) are from the *New Revised Standard Version of the Bible*, copyright 1989 by the Division of Christian Education of the National Council of the Churches of Christ in the USA. Used by permission.

Scripture quotations marked (GNB/TEV) are from the *Good News Bible*, in Today's English Version. Copyright © American Bible Society 1966, 1971, 1976. Used by permission.

Scripture quotations marked (RSV) are from the *Revised Standard Version of the Bible*, copyrighted 1946, 1952 ©, 1971, 1973, by the Division of Christian Education of the National Council of the Churches of Christ in the USA. Used by permission.

Scripture quotations marked (TJB) are excerpts from *The Jerusalem Bible*, copyright © 1966 by Darton, Longman & Todd, Ltd., and Doubleday, a division of Bantam Doubleday Dell Publishing Group, Inc., Reprinted by permission.

For more information about CSS Publishing Company resources, visit our website at www.csspub.com or e-mail us at custserv@csspub.com or call (800) 241-4056.

ISBN 0-7880-2304-7

Contents

Preface

Many changes in worship have taken place since *Come, Follow Me* was published in 1982. One such change is that many more churches have acolytes. Even some pastors and congregations which once looked on acolytes as "high church" have discovered the value of having young people assist in worship.

Unfortunately, this does not mean that these acolytes know what they are doing or why they are doing it or that they are doing all they might do. In far too many cases, the acolytes are untrained and simply go through meaningless motions. When asked why they are doing what they are doing, they say, "Because that lady told me to."

And in many cases, acolytes do nothing except light and extinguish the candles. In fact, in some churches acolytes don't extinguish the candles because they have not stayed for the worship service. Sometimes, they are not even on church property! They have lighted the candles and gone home.

WHAT A WASTE of youthful energy, intelligence, and devotion! WHAT A MISSED OPPORTUNITY to involve young people in meaningful service to Christ and the Church!

The purpose of this study book is to provide pastors with a tool for helping acolytes understand the meaning of worship and the valuable service acolytes can render in worship. *Come, Follow Me* began over thirty years ago as a series of mimeographed sheets given to my acolytes one topic at a time. Finally, these pages were pulled together, revised, expanded, shared with other pastors, and revised further until they were ready for a wider audience.

Now, it is time to revise the material again. This revision 1) updates some of the material, especially that referring to the Order of Worship and the Christian Year; 2) rearranges the chapters so that more concrete concepts are dealt with first and more abstract concepts later; 3) provides an expanded section for pastors; 4) provides some quizzes and tests which can be used "as is" or as a starting point for the pastor to prepare his/her own; and 5) includes a service of consecration shared with me by the Reverend Dr. Timothy Weitkamp.

This study book is written with seventh and eighth graders in mind. I hope it is simple enough for them to understand. However, I assume that you will interpret, expand, illustrate, and apply the material as it applies to your particular situation. If your acolytes are younger than seventh grade, you may need to "translate" the text into simpler language.

I purposely include repetition in the text because I think this is one way people learn. The sections on "How Much Do You Remember?" are intended for review. In addition, I have added some quizzes and tests which can be used "as is" or modified to meet your needs. However, the intended purpose of these quizzes and tests is not to pass or fail acolytes, but to help them learn and to hold them accountable for their learning.

Since I have not changed my theology of worship, the content of those sections has not changed, though some ways of expressing that content may have changed. But since I have been a United Methodist pastor for over forty years, I am sure that bias will show, especially in my references to church history, the order of worship, and worship resources. I trust pastors of other traditions will include references to their own history, order of worship, and worship resources in addition to (or instead of) what I have said.

I am indebted to Tim Weitkamp for serving as "mid-husband" on this project. He has motivated and encouraged me, shared and tested ideas, and read the revised text before it was sent to the publisher. If it had not been for Tim, this revision would not have happened. I am grateful to him. I hope you are, too.

Ed Womack

Notes To Pastors

This study book for acolytes is the distillation of working with and writing for acolytes for **over thirty years**. When I first began an acolyte program in 1960, I looked for printed material to help me. I found some booklets on how to organize a group and others concerning what acolytes should do in the sanctuary, but I could find nothing which would help me teach acolytes the **meaning** of worship and **why** they do what they do. So, I wrote my own. At first, I mimeographed information sheets for my acolytes. These sheets were revised and expanded, shared with other pastors, and revised further. After eighteen years, I prepared the material for publication, and *Come, Follow Me* was printed in 1982. Now, after fifteen years of use and more comments from other pastors, it is revised again.

MY BIAS

I have been a **United Methodist local pastor** for over forty years, so I write from that bias. However, I hope this material will be helpful to pastors and acolytes of any denomination. If you come from a different tradition or disagree with what I say, *I trust you will modify or add to this material as needed.*

All of my ministry has been in the **western United States** (Arizona, Hawaii, and California), and most of it has been in rural churches varying in membership from 100 to 315. I served one urban church of 1,200 members. I retired four years ago.

I believe **the worship of God is the most important thing Christians do**. It is the basis of all of our other ministries, and it involves more "people hours" per week than any other activity of the church. Therefore, worship should be very carefully planned and led. That does not mean that worship must be "formal," rigid, pompous, or boring. It does mean that worship should be dignified and reverent, that worship should focus upon God rather than upon ourselves, and that worship leaders should be carefully instructed and trained. It is with this understanding of worship that this study book is written.

THE IMPORTANCE OF ACOLYTES

I become angry when people refer to acolytes as "those sweet little children who light the candles on Sunday morning." Acolytes do not have to be little; very often they are not sweet; they can do much more than light candles; and their work does not need to be restricted to Sunday morning.

Properly instructed, acolytes can be very effective worship leaders. But proper instruction in both the physical actions expected of acolytes *and* the meaning of what they are doing takes time, effort, energy, and patience. *So, why bother?*

Acolytes are important because **they can enrich the worship experience** for everyone. In a rural church I served forty years ago, the usher lighted the candles by striking a match on the seat of his pants. I prefer an acolyte using a candlelighter. I think the congregation does, too.

Acolytes are important because **they can be very helpful assistants to the pastor**. During a baptism, I appreciate having an acolyte hold my service book rather than having to rest it on the communion rail. In one church I served, we used individual cups for Holy Communion, and the communion rail was over twenty feet from the altar. Having acolytes bring the bread and wine to me saved over fifteen minutes in the service. Both the congregation and I were grateful. And I still remember sending an acolyte to my study to retrieve my sermon notes while I continued with the worship service.

Acolytes are important because of **what happens to the young people**. Many (if not most) churches are adult oriented and have few places where young people can be involved in meaningful, helpful service that gives them importance and helps them grow in faith and in church leadership. An acolyte program can provide such an opportunity. It may even give acolytes an opportunity to learn things their parents and other adults have never heard of. When parishioners ask questions about the sanctuary, symbols, the Christian Year, and other things acolytes have learned, acolytes make good teachers — and they enjoy it.

Being an acolyte should involve **serious commitment**. This book lists some of the disciplines expected of an acolyte. You may want to add to or subtract from the list. But, being an acolyte should call for faithful service to Christ and the Church and be a natural step to the commitment of confirmation and church membership.

THE PASTOR AND ACOLYTES

We pastors are busy people and our time is precious. I know that. I've been there! But I am convinced that the pastor should be in charge of the acolyte program, even in a large church. This is a **rare opportunity** for the pastor to work with a small, disciplined group of youth, who, at an early age,

1. learn that the pastor is a friend and teacher who will spend time with them to help them grow in wisdom and faith,

2. learn meanings of worship which will remain with them for life, and

3. become involved in meaningful service to Christ and his Church and look forward to other areas of service, including church-related vocations.

If we are honest about being pastor to the entire congregation, then we should be willing to spend time with young people. And if we expect serious commitment from our young people, they should expect equally serious commitment from us. I think it is wise to have lay helpers to handle some of the routine non-teaching details of the acolyte program, but I think pastors should be the main teacher of acolytes. Of course, it will involve time, energy, and frustration on your part. But **it is worth it!**

Finally, a word of caution about the special responsibility we have to our youth. As I write this (Fall, 2002), newspapers and television news programs are full of headlines, articles, and sound bites about pastors and priests abusing boys and girls who are under their guidance. Therefore, I must include a word about our ethical behavior toward young people.

Pastors have the great and grave responsibility of shaping the lives of young people entrusted to our care. Our Lord was very blunt about the seriousness of causing a "little one" to sin. "It would be better for him if a great millstone were hung around his neck and he were thrown into the sea" (Mark 9:42 RSV).

The Church, at every level, must do everything possible to ensure that its pastors never harm a child or even give the appearance of harming a child. Therefore, as we relate to our acolytes, we must do at least three things.

First, we must be sure that our words and actions carry no sexual overtones, even in jest.

Second, if we need to speak privately with a child, we should do so in a place where we can be seen, though not heard, by others.

Third, whenever we meet with young people, another adult, preferably one of the opposite sex, should be present. This person might help with instruction and training, serve refreshments, or provide general supervision. But, regardless of whatever else he or she might do, she or he is also a witness to the fact that nothing improper is happening.

I regret that this word of caution is necessary. But we live in a world where many are suspicious, fearful, and litigious and where some pastoral leaders have abused children. Therefore, taking the time and effort to be a bit more careful could prove to be very important to you, your acolytes, the congregation, and the Church.

ACOLYTES IN CONTEMPORARY WORSHIP

What is the place, if any, of acolytes in contemporary worship? Are acolytes so associated with "traditional" worship that a church which is worshiping in a "contemporary" style should *automatically* exclude the use of acolytes? I hope not.

"Traditional" worship and "contemporary" worship are *not* mutually exclusive forms of worship. The *purpose* of worship is the same — to declare that nothing is more important than God. Many of the same *acts of worship* — hymns, scripture, sermon, prayers, sacraments, offering, and special music — are used in both styles of worship. *Visual forms of worship* — symbols, candles, paraments, banners, and stained-glass windows — can enrich contemporary worship as well as traditional worship.

Therefore, whether the worship setting is formal or informal, whether or not there is a printed order of worship, whether hymns are read from a book or from a screen, whether music is led by a praise band or an organ, whether the pastor stands in the center of the chancel or behind a pulpit, makes little or no difference. **There may still be a place for acolytes.**
- If candles are used as symbols of the presence of Christ, someone must light and extinguish the candles.
- If there is a baptism, someone needs to open and close the baptismal font, and it may be helpful for a helper to hold the service book or hymnal so that it doesn't get wet.

- If Holy Communion is served, someone may need to supply the servers with bread and wine.
- If the pastor forgets the sermon notes, it might be handy to have someone to fetch them.

So, in either traditional or contemporary worship, acolytes can enrich the worship service, help the pastor, and grow in faith and commitment as they learn to be faithful disciples and worship leaders.

It may require some extra thoughts and effort on the part of those planning worship, **but it will be worth it!**

HOW DO WE DO IT?

There are various ways to develop an acolyte program, and **you need to find a way that fits** your personality and your style and meets the needs of the congregation. Here are two very different examples which show how two different pastors — Ed Womack and Tim Weitkamp — have done it.

Weekly Meetings

I prefer to work with **seventh and eighth graders** because their attention span is longer, they can deal with more abstract concepts, and often (not always!) they are more responsible. But I have had acolytes as young as the fourth grade and as old as the eleventh grade.

I **recruit acolytes** by personal invitation, enlisting only the number I can use effectively. Acolytes who are faithful in study and service are allowed to serve for two years. Then they are expected to leave the program to make room for someone else.

They serve in the sanctuary every other week. (Weekly service wears them out and interferes with family schedules; serving less often is not often enough to keep them interested in coming to class.)

I **meet with the acolytes** for one hour each week, usually after school, except during summer vacation. The hour is divided into thirds — 20 minutes to **study**, discuss problems, and set the serving schedule; 20 minutes to **practice** in the sanctuary; and 20 minutes for **refreshments** (furnished by acolyte parents).

We use *Come, Follow Me* as the **study book** and take it very slowly, with a lot of repetition, moving to a new chapter only when the acolytes are comfortable with what they already have learned. Seventh and eighth graders complete the book in one year. Younger acolytes take two years.

One way to judge when to move to new material is to use **quizzes and tests**. These are never used to embarrass or fail an acolyte. They are used to help an acolyte learn what she/he already knows and what needs further attention. **Quizzes** are given after a time of review, but are not graded or recorded. **Tests** for awards require a grade of 85 percent or better (a very high standard!) but can be taken as many times as necessary. Reviewing for the test a second time helps the acolytes learn, while taking the same test provides some security for the student. I do not say to a student, "You failed the test." I say, "You didn't make 85." Very seldom is a test taken more than twice.

Everyone likes to be recognized for work done and progress made, so **public recognition** is part of the program. Since the pastor and choir wear vestments to cover their street clothes and to indicate that they are worship leaders, acolytes are vested for the same reasons. Also, acolytes are presented with appropriate pins or medallions on three different occasions: 1) when welcomed into service after passing a quiz on what an acolyte is and does, 2) when half of the course of study has been completed, and 3) when the course of study has been completed. These pins or medallions are presented during worship and are worn with the vestments. At the end of two years of service, an acolyte is thanked in worship and given a certificate of appreciation.

Another Possibility (an acolyte workshop)

Rather than have acolyte meetings throughout the school year, the Reverend Doctor Tim Weitkamp has a six-week workshop. Here is an outline of his plan.

I generally teach an acolyte workshop **once a year** if there is enough interest. I **recruit** students in grades 5, 6, and 7, using the newsletter, Sunday school, pulpit announcements, and sometimes, a personal letter. I like to have at least three students in the class to keep it more interesting.

The **workshop meets for six weeks**. Classes are held after school, last for about an hour, and include a snack — for the kids that is! (I have done the workshop during the Sunday school hour.)

We use *Come, Follow Me* as the **study book**, covering two chapters each week. The fifth week is devoted to "hands on" training. This session usually runs a bit longer. I have each acolyte go through everything he/she will be doing in the worship service (i.e., actually lighting and extinguishing candles, distributing offering plates, etc.). The final week is for review and the **final quiz**. This includes a "Practice Quiz," which is exactly the same as the final quiz except for the title. But I do not tell the students this ahead of time. Also, I don't tell them ahead of time that a student who fails the test may retake it as often as necessary. I want them to take the review and the test seriously, but I am more interested in their knowing the material than passing or failing. (A copy of Tim's final test is included in the section on Tests.)

The acolyte serving schedule is made up for six months at a time. This way, acolytes can plan ahead for when they will serve, and if a new class is formed, the new acolytes can be placed in the rotation fairly easily.

During their time of serving, I try to praise the acolytes as much as possible. I lift up their importance to me and to the worshiping community. They are always seated in a prominent place in the chancel area. When they "retire" from service, they are recognized with a certificate and a gift during the worship service.

DO WHAT WORKS FOR YOU

These two examples show that there is more than one way to have an effective acolyte program. How you develop the program depends upon your church tradition, your congregational needs, what you want to accomplish with an acolyte program, and what you want and are able to do. You need to **develop a program that works for you and your church**.

On the other hand, these examples also show that there are some **essential elements** to any effective acolyte program:
- determine the needs of the pastor and congregation
- recruit the needed acolytes
- provide for regular study and practice
- demand commitment and faithfulness
- set a reasonable service schedule
- determine what kind of dress is appropriate
- give appropriate public recognition
- enjoy your time with a great bunch of kids!

AN OFFICE FOR THE CONSECRATION OF ACOLYTES
(a gift from Tim Wietkamp)

(Acolyte candidates shall come forward and stand at the chancel rail at the appointed time.)

Minister to the congregation: I present to you these persons who have been duly trained and are qualified to be consecrated as acolytes for service in the house of God. (Here you may substitute the name of your church.)

(Minister shall examine the candidates.)

Minister: Do you believe in your heart that you have been led by the Spirit of God to assume the responsibilities of an acolyte?

Acolytes: I do so believe.

Minister: Will you strive to carry out faithfully the responsibilities and duties of an acolyte to the glory of God and the service of his holy Church?

Acolytes: I will, the Lord being my helper.

Minister: Will you follow the Lord Jesus as your teacher and ruler of your life?

Acolytes: I will.

Minister: Will you do all in your power to live before God and this congregation a life that demonstrates true Christian discipleship?

Acolytes: I will, by God's grace.

Minister: Will you be loyal to the (United Methodist) Church and uphold it by your prayers, your presence, your gifts, and your service?

Acolytes: I will.

Laying on of Hands
The minister shall have the acolytes kneel and, placing his hands upon the head of each one, shall repeat these words:

Minister: (Name), I consecrate you as an acolyte in the (United Methodist) Church in the name of the Father, the Son, and the Holy Spirit. Amen.

Presentation of the Cross (Optional)
A cross or acolyte necklace may be presented to each acolyte to be worn whenever serving.

(Acolytes then stand and face the congregation.)

Address to the Congregation
Minister: Brothers and sisters of the household of faith, I commend to you these young people who have been consecrated for service in the church as acolytes. Do all in your power to assist them in fulfilling their duties and to increase their faith.

Congregation: We rejoice with you this day and recognize you as acolytes in our church. We will seek to support you through our love and prayers.

Prayer by the Pastor

Hymn: "Take My Life, And Let It Be"

QUIZZES AND TESTS

You may want to use quizzes and tests to encourage review, to mark progress, to hold acolytes accountable for learning, and to indicate readiness for recognition.

Usually **quizzes** are brief and informal. Sometimes they are unannounced. In any case, they need to **fit your group**. So I encourage you to make your own quizzes. If you need questions, look at each "How Much Do You Remember?" and the chapter tests.

I have provided two **tests** for each chapter. Test "A" is for younger students and includes mostly "recognition questions" — true-false and multiple choice. Test "B" includes more "recall questions" — completion or essay. There is also a test which covers the first half of the book, a "final exam" that covers the entire book, and Tim Weitkamp's final test for the acolyte workshop. I trust you will use, modify, or ignore these according to your own wisdom.

A FINAL WORD

I assume you are a busy pastor with more to do than can be done. So, is a creative, meaningful acolyte program worth the effort? **Yes!** As I look back on my ministry, working with acolytes has been one of the most enjoyable and most rewarding things I have done. It has been worth all of the time, energy, and frustration it required, and I am sure it will be worth it for you, too.

May God richly bless you and your acolytes as you worship and work and serve God together. Amen.

Ed Womack

Welcome To Acolytes

I'm glad you have chosen to become an acolyte. You have decided to share in one of the most important services a young person can render to the worship life of the Church.

Some people think of acolytes as "cute little kids who light the candles" — and then disappear. I hope that won't be true of you. You can do much more than light candles, and your work is far too important for you to remain hidden.

But if you are going to enjoy your work and if your service is going to be most helpful to the pastor and the congregation

YOU NEED TO KNOW WHAT YOU ARE DOING.

Who wants to go through a lot of meaningless motions?
Who wants to waste time on unimportant things?
NOT YOU, I'm sure.

But **if you know what you are doing**, your service can be enjoyable, and it can have a deep meaning which will last long after you have stopped serving as an acolyte.

The purpose of this book is to help you know what you are doing. I hope it will help you understand
- what an acolyte is;
- the kinds of things acolytes do;
- why they do these things;
- what habits they should form.

Since you will be serving in public worship, you need to know
- what worship is;
- how different churches worship.

Since you will be involved with Christian symbols, you need to know
- what symbols are;
- what different symbols represent;
- how symbols help us worship.

Since you will be serving during different seasons of the Christian Year, you need to know
- where our festivals and seasons came from;
- how they should be celebrated;
- how they can help us worship;
- how they can help us grow in faith.

Since you will be following an order of worship, you need to know
- what an order of worship is;
- what different acts of worship do;
- how the order of service is put together.

1

Since you may be helping with the sacraments, you need to know
- what a sacrament is;
- what each sacrament means;
- why sacraments are important.

I hope this manual will give you some important information about all of these things. And if you learn well, I am sure your service as an acolyte will be much more meaningful.

But, **this manual cannot tell you everything** you need to know. That would be impossible. The book would be far too long — and far too boring. You would never finish reading it.

Besides, acolytes serve in different ways in different churches, and pastors differ in the ways they want acolytes to serve. So this manual will **not** tell you how to do specific things such as
- light and extinguish candles,
- carry the cross or banner,
- assist with Holy Baptism or Holy Communion,
- help with the offering,
- assist at weddings or funerals.

These **actions** are determined by
- the arrangement of the house of worship,
- the desires of your pastor, and
- the worship needs of your congregation.

SO, YOUR PASTOR WILL TEACH YOU THOSE THINGS.

Your pastor will teach you **what** he or she wants done and **how** you are to do it. This book will help you understand **why** you are doing what you do.

WELL, ARE YOU READY?

Then, let's begin by finding out what an acolyte **is**, some of the things acolytes **do**, and how acolytes are expected to **act**.

What Is An Acolyte?

Acolyte is a strange sounding word. You seldom hear it except in church. What does it mean?

We have borrowed many words from other languages. For example, "restaurant" is French; "patio" is Spanish; "smorgasbord" is Swedish; and "wiener" is German. We have also borrowed from the ancient languages of GREEK and LATIN.

"Acolyte" is one of the words we have borrowed from the Greek language. The Greek word is **akolouthos** (pronounced ahKAH-loo-thahs). When you change the Greek letters into English letters it comes out like this:

$$\alpha \quad \kappa \quad o \quad \lambda \quad o \quad \upsilon \quad \theta \quad o \quad s$$
$$a \quad k \quad o \quad l \quad o \quad u \quad th \quad o \quad s$$
$$a \quad c \quad o \quad l \quad \quad \quad y \quad t$$

Then we put the "e" on the end.

BUT WHAT DOES IT MEAN? **Akolouthos** comes from the Greek verb meaning **to follow**. Therefore, an acolyte is someone who follows someone else, a FOLLOWER. The verb is used many times in the New Testament. Four passages in which it is used are printed below. I suggest that you memorize them. They are good verses to repeat before you enter the sanctuary on Sunday morning.

> Jesus said, "I am the light of the world; whoever **follows** me will never walk in darkness but will have the light of life."   — John 8:12 (NRSV)

> Jesus said, "My sheep hear my voice. I know them, and they **follow** me. I give them eternal life."   — John 10:27 (NRSV)

> Jesus said, "**Follow** me, and I will make you fish for people." Immediately they left their nets and **followed** him.   — Matthew 4:19-20 (NRSV)

> Jesus said, "If any want to become my followers, let them deny themselves and take up their cross and **follow** me."   — Mark 8:34 (NRSV)

Christians are **followers** of Jesus Christ. Therefore, in one sense, all Christians are acolytes of Jesus Christ. And that is the most important thing an acolyte does — follow Jesus.

But that is not all there is to it. Because those who follow someone else usually try to help the person they follow, the word **acolyte** is often translated as HELPER or ASSISTANT. That is the way we usually use the word in the church. An acolyte is a person who helps the pastor in public worship.

Put these two ideas together, and you have a good definition of **acolyte** as we use it in the Church today.

An acolyte is a person who 1) follows Jesus Christ as Lord and 2) in service to Christ, helps the pastor in public worship.

Notice that the definition has two parts. Both parts are necessary. Leave out either part and the definition is incomplete.

And notice the order. First, you follow Jesus. Then you help the pastor. Helping the pastor in worship is one way of serving Christ.

THE DUTIES OF AN ACOLYTE

Some people do not like the word "duty." Maybe they have had an experience where duties made them feel bad. Or, maybe, they do not understand what a duty is.

A DUTY IS A TASK WHICH IS REQUIRED OF SOMEONE WORKING IN A PARTICULAR JOB. While you are "on the job," certain things are expected of you. When you are "off duty," they are not expected. For example:

One DUTY of a secretary is to type letters for the employer. But he does that only while at work. After work, he is not expected to do that.

One DUTY of a policeman is to direct traffic. But she does that only while "on duty." After work, that is not expected.

NOW, WHAT'S SO BAD ABOUT THAT?

Acolytes have duties, too. There are certain things you will be expected to do while serving as an acolyte. Exactly what those duties are depends upon 1) what needs to be done and 2) what the pastor wants you to do.

Here are some things that are expected of acolytes in many churches:
1. Attend acolyte classes regularly
2. Prepare class assignments on time
3. Be faithful in serving at the appointed time
4. Take proper care of vestments and equipment
5. Dress properly for service in the sanctuary
6. Check the sanctuary before worship (to be sure everything is properly prepared)
7. Light candles at the beginning of the service
8. Extinguish candles at the end of the service
9. Carry the processional banner or cross
10. Carry the Bible or hold it while it is read
11. Assist the pastor during Holy Baptism
12. Assist the pastor during Holy Communion
13. Assist the pastor at weddings or funerals
14. Run errands for the pastor
15. Assist visiting pastors

I do not know of any church where acolytes are expected to do ALL of those things ALL the time. And some acolytes may do things I have not listed. PUT A CHECK MARK BY EACH THING YOUR PASTOR EXPECTS ACOLYTES TO DO IN YOUR CHURCH.

THE DISCIPLINES OF AN ACOLYTE

Here is another word some people do not like — DISCIPLINE. Maybe that is because they associate discipline with punishment. That is one meaning of the word, and if that were the only meaning, I wouldn't like the word either.

But, have you ever heard the word **disciple**? That's not a bad word, and it comes from the same root as discipline. Both mean **teaching**. A discipline is something that teaches us, and a disciple is someone who learns. So, you can think of a discipline as A HABIT WE LEARN WHICH MAKES LIFE WHAT WE WANT IT TO BE.

So, duties and disciplines are not the same thing, and we need to understand the difference.

A **duty** is a TASK required by a particular job.
A **discipline** is a HABIT that shapes our life.

Therefore, we carry out the duties of an acolyte only while serving as an acolyte, but disciplines are LIFE HABITS we do all the time.

Now, what kind of habits do you need to form if you are going to assist your pastor in public worship? Let me name a few. Your pastor may want to add to the list.

1. Follow Jesus as the ruler of your life.
2. Set a good example for others to follow.
3. Be reverent in the house of worship at all times.
4. Be regular in public worship even when not serving.
5. Be on time.
6. Be clean and neat in personal appearance (especially when serving in the sanctuary).
7. Wash your hands before assisting with Holy Communion.
8. Behave properly during worship.
9. Be courteous and respectful.
10. Be faithful in carrying out the duties assigned to you.

Let me stress three of these disciplines.

> FOLLOW JESUS AS THE RULER OF YOUR LIFE. Remember that following Jesus is more important than assisting the pastor in worship. So, if you do not act like a follower of Jesus, people will wonder why you are an acolyte.
>
> SET A GOOD EXAMPLE FOR OTHERS TO FOLLOW. As an acolyte, you serve in public. People know who you are. They see what you do — in church and away from church. **Children** are watching you and looking up to you and

saying to themselves, "Whatever he (she) does must be okay because he (she) is an acolyte." So, be careful!

BEHAVE PROPERLY IN WORSHIP. Your pastor will tell you how he (she) expects you to act in worship, but remember that if you chew gum, blow bubbles, walk sloppily, slump down in your seat, talk during prayers, or don't pay attention, people get the message that you think worship is unimportant. Is that the message you want to send?

Please watch all of your disciplines. Strengthen your good habits, and get rid of the bad ones. You will be a better acolyte. You will be a better person.

WELL, THAT IS SOMETHING OF WHAT IT MEANS TO BE AN ACOLYTE.
Does it sound important? I hope so. **It is.**
Does it sound a little scary? I hope not.
YOU CAN DO IT!

Otherwise, you would not have been chosen to be an acolyte. And you do not have to do it all at once. Take one step at a time. You will find it an exciting adventure. But don't get lazy. And don't get careless.

YOU HAVE IMPORTANT WORK TO DO!
YOU ARE AN IMPORTANT SERVANT OF CHRIST AND HIS CHURCH!
FOLLOW FAITHFULLY!
SERVE WELL!

HOW MUCH DO YOU REMEMBER?

True or False

    T   F   An acolyte is any person who follows Jesus.

    T   F   Acolyte comes from a LATIN word meaning FISHERMAN.

    T   F   Acolytes in different churches do different jobs.

    T   F   Duties are tasks required for a certain job.

    T   F   Duties and disciplines are the same thing.

    T   F   "Disciple" and "discipline" come from the same root.

Which statements are included in the definition of an acolyte?
1. follows Jesus Christ as Lord
2. is a member of the church
3. is fifteen years old
4. helps the pastor in public worship
5. must be good looking
6. lights candles
7. wears a funny-looking uniform
8. helps the pastor in order to have fun
9. helps the pastor in order to serve Christ

List (from memory) four DUTIES your pastor expects of you.

_____

_____

_____

_____

List (from memory) three DISCIPLINES of any acolyte.

_____

_____

_____

Write (from memory) two passages from the New Testament which use *akolouthos.*

_____

_____

_____

_____

_____

_____

_____

_____

The House Of Worship

Most of your service as an acolyte will take place in the house of worship. Therefore, you need to become familiar with the "geography" of that house. Otherwise, you may find it difficult to follow certain instructions.

If the pastor says, "I will meet you in the narthex," you will not know where to go unless you know what the narthex is.

Or, if she says, "Please check the chancel to see that everything is ready for the worship service," how will you know what to check if you don't know where the chancel is?

To know what these words mean, you need to learn the different parts of the house of worship.

Churches are built in many different shapes and sizes — big, little, rectangular, round, cross-shaped. Some are very plain. Others are very ornate. That's okay. All churches do not have to be the same. But even with all of these differences, MOST HOUSES OF WORSHIP HAVE FOUR PARTS, each with its own special function and name.

The "outer court" or entrance way is called the **NARTHEX**. It is like an enclosed porch. **In the early church**, it served a very special function. EVERYONE was allowed to participate in the service of the Word — singing hymns, hearing the scriptures read, listening to instruction, and offering prayers. But only those who had been BAPTIZED could share in the service of Holy Communion. Those who had *not* been baptized left the service, went to the NARTHEX, watched the baptized Christians share in the Lord's Supper, and looked forward to the time when they had finished their instruction in the faith and could share in the sacrament.

Today, the NARTHEX usually is used only as an enclosed entrance to the house of worship. But it is more than a place to get out of the weather, take off your coat, and say, "Good morning!" to someone. This is where we make the transition **from** the noise of the street **to** the quietness of the church, **from** the problems of the day **to** the reverence of worship. So, when we enter the NARTHEX, we lower our voices or become silent so that we will not disturb others and so we can prepare ourselves for worship.

Leaving the narthex, we enter the main hall, which is called the **NAVE**. Nave is the Latin word for "ship." (We get our word "navy" from the same Latin word, because a navy is made up of ships.) Many early churches were long and narrow, with high walls and pointed ceilings. (Many today are, too.) If you were to turn them over, you might think you were in a ship. So this part of the house of worship is called "the ship" — the NAVE. This is where the congregation gathers for worship, the area with the seats or pews.

In the front of the nave is the **CHANCEL**. This is the area from which worship is led. Often, it is a raised platform. This makes it easier for people to see and hear the worship leaders.

A long time ago, the CHANCEL was reserved only for the clergy, and barriers were put up to keep lay people out. Since the Latin word for "crossbars" is "chancel," this area was called the CHANCEL.

Today, in many churches, lay people help lead worship from the CHANCEL, and it is separated from the nave only by a low wooden wall called a **chancel rail**. Sometimes, it is called the **communion rail** because people kneel here to receive the sacrament. Other churches have no dividing rail at all, and we say that they have **open chancels**.

Inside the CHANCEL is the furniture used for conducting worship. Very often, you will find the:
- pulpit (a raised platform from which the pastor preaches)
- lectern (a reading stand from which the Bible is read)
- chairs (for pastors, liturgists, and acolytes)

Some churches have a pulpit, but no lectern. Other churches include the choir and the organ in the chancel.

Because the CHANCEL is the area from which worship is led, it is **a special place**. When you are in the chancel, you need to watch your behavior in a special way. It is a place for leaders — **worship** leaders. Be sure that everything you do in the chancel is a good example for others to follow.

Time for a spelling lesson! There is a big difference between CHANCEL and CANCEL.

CHANCEL is a part of the house of worship.
CANCEL means "to cross out" or "to do away with."

Keep them straight! It makes a difference!

At, or near, the front of the house of worship is the **SANCTUARY**. This is the focal point of the room. Everything points toward it. Here we find the main symbols of our faith:

- the **cross** which reminds us of Jesus' sacrificial love;
- the **candles** which remind us that Christ is the light of the world;
- the **altar** which reminds us of the sacrifice Christ made for us and of the sacrifices we should make for him;
- the **communion table** which reminds us of Jesus' death and resurrection and of our fellowship with him and other Christians.

THIS IS THE PART OF THE BUILDING WHICH HELPS US REMEMBER
WHO GOD IS
AND
WHAT GOD HAS DONE
TO GIVE US GOD'S LOVE.

The word SANCTUARY means "a safe place." **In Bible times**, if a person *accidentally* killed someone and the victim's family tried to avenge the death before a fair trial could be held, the killer could run to the temple, hold on to the altar, and be safe. Those who were after him could not kill him there. The altar was his SANCTUARY, his safe place. (Note: A murderer who killed someone *on purpose* was not allowed sanctuary at the altar.) **Today**, we speak of a "bird sanctuary" as a place where birds cannot be hunted or killed. We also think of the altar in the church as a sacred place where we can be safe in the presence of God. In fact, because the altar is there, we think of the whole church as a place to find help in times of trouble.

The most prominent piece of furniture in the SANCTUARY is the **altar** or **communion table**. Because the altar is so important, sometimes this area of the house of worship is called the ALTAR as well as the SANCTUARY.

An altar is a *place of sacrifice*. **In Bible times**, a Jew who was very thankful for good things he had received, or was very sorry for something bad he had done, would go to the Temple in Jerusalem to offer a sacrifice of something which was valuable to him. Usually, it was an ox, a ram, some grain, or some wine. But whatever he offered, it was always the BEST that he had. **Today**, when we come to give God thanks and to offer ourselves in service to God, we bring something valuable — our money and our lives — to the altar, to *the place of sacrifice*, and offer them to God. Let's be sure we always bring God our BEST.

> *"Offer yourselves as a living sacrifice to God, dedicated to his service and pleasing to him. This is the true worship you should offer."* — Romans 12:1 (TEV)

In most Protestant churches, the only difference between an altar and a communion table is the way they are made. Most altars do not have legs and look something like a large box. Most communion tables do have legs and look like tables. BOTH are used for receiving the gifts of the people and for holding the elements of bread and wine for the sacrament of Holy Communion. In some churches, ONLY sacrificial items are allowed on the altar or communion table.

Time for another spelling lesson! There is a big difference between ALTAR and ALTER.

ALTAR means "a place of sacrifice."
ALTER means "to change."

Keep them straight! It makes a difference!

Because the SANCTUARY is the most important part of the house of worship, it **lends its name** to the entire building used for worship. You will hear people say,

> "Let's go into the sanctuary for worship."
>   or
> "The conference will be held in the sanctuary."

They really do not intend for everyone to sit around the altar for worship or for the conference. They mean that you are to go into the room that *has* the altar or communion table.

It's really not as confusing as you might think. Know that the word is used both ways and listen carefully, and you will know what people mean.

So, most houses of worship are divided into four parts
- the NARTHEX
- the NAVE
- the CHANCEL
- the SANCTUARY

Study the way your house of worship is built. Learn where the different parts are found. Then visit other churches to see how they are built. It is an interesting and enjoyable way to learn about worship.

HOW MUCH DO YOU REMEMBER?

True or False

T	F	All churches are built in the same way and look alike.
T	F	A church shaped like a cross is better than one which is round or square.
T	F	In the early church, everyone could share in the service of the Word, but only baptized Christians could share in Holy Communion.
T	F	NAVE comes from the Greek word for "ox cart."
T	F	The chancel is always separated from the nave by a low rail.
T	F	The communion table usually is in the narthex.
T	F	Chairs for worship leaders usually are in the chancel.
T	F	Sanctuary means "a safe place."
T	F	Altar means "communion table."

Draw a line **from** the part of the house of worship **to** its proper description.

SANCTUARY	entrance way
CHANCEL	where the congregation sits
NARTHEX	area with the altar or communion table
NAVE	area from which worship is led

Draw a simple floor plan of your house of worship and locate the narthex, the nave, the chancel, and the sanctuary. (Use a separate piece of paper if you need more room.)

Christian Symbols

Symbols are all around us. We see them and use them every day, often without even realizing it. A "+" means "add to" and a "-" sign means "take away." A red light means "STOP" and a green light means, "GO." My typewriter has a lot of symbols on it — ! ? # $ % ¢ & *. Many computers have symbols or "icons" you can "click on" to give the computer instructions.

A SYMBOL is an object or form which **represents** or **reminds** us of some
  - person,
      - event,
          - idea, or
              - thing.

A *ring* worn on the third finger of the left hand **reminds** us of marriage promises. A *flag* fluttering in the breeze **represents** our nation. *Bread* and *wine* on the altar **remind** us of the death and resurrection of Jesus. A *cross* worn around the neck **reminds** us that we belong to Christ.

Another word for symbol is SIGN, because a sign is something that **points to** something else.

The sign says,

STAY AT THE BROADWAY HOTEL
FIFTH STREET AT MAIN

The sign does not look like the hotel. You cannot get a room at the sign. The sign **points to** THE BROADWAY HOTEL. Go to the hotel to spend the night.

Another sign says,

SPEED LIMIT
55 MILES PER HOUR

You do not have to obey the sign. It is only steel and paint. But you **are** expected to obey the LAW which the sign **points to**.

Sometimes we confuse symbols with pictures. **Symbols are not the same as pictures.**

A PICTURE **looks like** the object, person, or scene it portrays.
A SYMBOL only **represents** it.

For example, many artists have painted pictures of Jesus' crucifixion and resurrection. The pictures include people, trees, rocks, and light, because the artist tried to paint what the crucifixion or resurrection might have looked like. But the cross in the chancel makes no attempt to show what the event looked like. It only **represents** or **reminds** us of the death and resurrection of our Lord.

Because symbols don't have to look like the objects they represent, they can be used to represent things which are impossible to picture.

> You can't draw a picture of the TRINITY, but you can **symbolize** it with an equilateral triangle.

> You can't draw a picture of LOVE, but you can **symbolize** it with a heart with an arrow through it.

> You can't draw a picture of our entire NATION, but you can **symbolize** it with thirteen stripes and fifty stars.

SYMBOLS AND WORSHIP

Symbols are *not necessary* for worship. You can worship without them. Many churches do. Some churches are even "anti-symbols." But, in the same way that maps *help* us study geography and drawings *help* us study science, symbols can *help* us worship. They help in three ways. Symbols

- provide a **visual** expression of our faith;
- let us worship with our **eyes** as well as our ears and mouths;
- help us **focus** attention by providing something to look at.

Many of the symbols used in churches today have been used for centuries and are used in churches all around the world. If you know their meaning, your worship can be more enjoyable and more meaningful wherever you are.

Probably the best way to study symbols is to tour your house of worship with your pastor, see the symbols used there, and have your pastor explain their meanings. Then, visit other churches to see what symbols they use and how they use them.

I suggest that you learn to **read symbols** by viewing them as groups and letting their meanings combine to make a **story**.

For example:

> **in the chancel**, an altar might hold a cross, two candles, and the altar flowers and be covered with a green cloth which is embroidered with an Alpha/Omega

> **the symbols involved** include
> - candles = light
> - two candles = Jesus is Son of God and Son of Man
> - altar = place of sacrifice
> - cross = death and resurrection of Christ; sacrificial love
> - flowers = resurrection
> - Alpha/Omega = beginning and end
> - green = growth

13

the **story** can read: Jesus of Nazareth, who is God's Son in human form, is the light of the world. He loved us enough to give his life for us, and God raised him from the dead. He is the beginning and end of our faith, and we should spread his message to all people.

Try this in your own house of worship. Look at the symbols in the chancel, on the walls, on the furniture, in the windows — wherever they are! Find out what each symbol means. Then fit them together into a story. Its fun! And it will help you worship.

SOME COMMON CHRISTIAN SYMBOLS

It would be impossible to show and describe here all of the Christian symbols in use. It would take hundreds of pages. So we will illustrate only those which are used very often and in many different ways. Learning these symbols will be a good basis for learning others as you see them in use. If you would like more information on symbols, ask your pastor to show you one of his/her books on symbols.

CROSS — Death and resurrection of Christ
God's love shown in the death and resurrection

LATIN CROSS — (three arms equal)

GREEK CROSS — (all arms equal)

TAU CROSS — (named for the Greek letter "T")

Note: all forms of the cross have the same meaning

 LAMP/CANDLE — Light; God is light
Jesus is the light of the world
    one light: Jesus is the light of the world
    two lights: Jesus is Son of God and Son of Man
    three lights: Holy Trinity; Father, Son, Holy Spirit
    six lights: the six days of creation
    seven lights: The Church; the gifts of the Holy Spirit

CHI RHO — Christ (a monogram made of the first two letters in the Greek word for Christ; pronounced "Kigh-row" or "Key-row")

IOTA ETA SIGMA	Jesus (a monogram made of the first three letters in the Greek word for Jesus)
ALPHA/OMEGA	Beginning and End (the first and last letters of the Greek alphabet)
FISH	Jesus Christ, God's Son, Savior (each word matches a letter in the Greek word for fish — i ch th u s)
DOVE	The Holy Spirit (when descending) Peace (when ascending or side-ways)
EQUILATERAL TRIANGLE	The Holy Trinity: Father, Son, and Holy Spirit
THREE EQUAL CIRCLES	The Holy Trinity: Father, Son, and Holy Spirit
CIRCLE	Eternal Life (no beginning or end)
EVERGREENS	Eternal Life (do not lose all needles at once)
BUTTERFLY	Resurrection (changing forms of life)
FLOWER	Resurrection (seed dies and gives new life)
HAND	God the Creator
SHIP	The Church
CROWN	King; Victory
LAMB	Sacrifice
STAR	Creation (with six points)

STAR   Nativity of Jesus (with five points)

 ANCHOR   Hope (an anchor holds firm)

 WHEAT   The Body of Christ; Holy Communion

GRAPES   The Blood of Christ; Holy Communion

Colors are used as symbols, too.

PURPLE   Royalty (once a very rare and expensive color)
                        Penitence (a somber color)

WHITE   Victory, Purity, Innocence

GREEN   Growth, Life, Faithfulness, Hope

RED   Blood, Martyrdom, Courage, Fire

HOW MUCH DO YOU REMEMBER?

True or False

T   F   A symbol reminds us of something.
T   F   Symbols are the same as pictures.
T   F   Symbols are used in mathematics and science.
T   F   Symbols are used only in churches.
T   F   We cannot worship without symbols.
T   F   Symbols help us worship by giving us something to see.
T   F   Symbols can remind us of things we cannot see.
T   F   The Latin cross and Greek cross have different meanings.
T   F   When we light candles we are dealing with symbols.
T   F   Alpha/Omega are letters from the Hebrew alphabet.
T   F   The butterfly symbolizes the resurrection of Jesus.
T   F   Iota Eta Sigma are English letters I H S.
T   F   To call Jesus "the lamb of God" is to remember his sacrifice.
T   F   In biblical times, purple cloth was very expensive.
T   F   Red stands for courage and martyrdom.

16

Beside each illustration, write the meaning of the symbol.

_____

_____

_____

_____

_____

_____

_____

_____

_____

_____

The Christian Year

How would you like to live without knowing what year, day, hour, or minute
  it is?
How would you like to live without calendars and clocks?
How would you like to live your whole life without a birthday party?
How would you like to graduate from high school with no celebration?

Human beings are very conscious of time. Not only do we live IN time, but we also find ingenious ways to keep track OF time. **Ancient people** carved holes in rocks to record and predict seasons. They made sundials and water clocks to measure hours and minutes.

Today, we use printed CALENDARS to help us remember years and days. We use CLOCKS and watches to help us remember hours and minutes. Some "time pieces" combine calendars and clocks to tell us the month and day of the year plus the hour, minute, and second of the day, and even have an alarm to tell us when a certain time has come.

We also have special times through CELEBRATIONS. Our **families** celebrate birthdays, weddings, graduations, and other special "times" in our lives. Our **nation** celebrates its independence, the end of wars, and the lives of great leaders. How dull life would be if we never had New Year's Day, the Fourth of July, Thanksgiving — or birthdays.

The Christian Church marks important events in its life by celebrating, too. In fact, we have a whole CALENDAR of festivals and seasons which is based on the main events in the life of Jesus and his Church. We call it **THE CHRISTIAN YEAR**.

Most of us are acquainted with **parts** of the Christian Year, such as Christmas and Easter. We also may know about Advent and Lent. What do you know about Epiphany and Pentecost?
                    What do they celebrate?
                    When do they come?
                    How long do they last?

Just as we need to learn how to read a CALENDAR to know when our birthday comes, and we need to learn how to read a CLOCK to know when to go to school, we need to learn how to use THE CHRISTIAN YEAR to know what we are celebrating in the life of Jesus and the Church.

CELEBRATING THE CHRISTIAN YEAR

Each festival and season of the Christian Year has a special **THEME**. For example, the theme of Christmas is that the Messiah is born, and the theme of Pentecost is that the Holy Spirit has come upon the Church. These themes are **ACTED OUT** or **CELEBRATED** in worship in various ways.

Perhaps your pastor chooses the **SCRIPTURE LESSONS** from the lectionary. "Lection" is the Latin word for "reading," so a lectionary is a list of Bible readings. Usually, the lectionary lists
  • an Old Testament reading,
      • an Epistle reading,

- a Gospel reading, and
- a Psalm

for each Sunday and special festival of the year. These readings were chosen according to the theme of the season, and they tell us about some special event in the life of Jesus.

Perhaps your pastor preaches **SERMONS** based on the lessons from the lectionary. If so, the sermon will express the theme of the season.

Often, **HYMNS** are chosen to fit the season. For example, "Silent Night" fits Christmas better than it fits Pentecost, and "Christ The Lord Is Risen Today" is more appropriate during Easter than during Epiphany.

PRAYERS and **RESPONSIVE READINGS** also may be written or chosen to express the theme of the season.

We can use **COLOR** to indicate the season. Does your church use cloths on the altar, pulpit, and lectern? Does your pastor wear a stole around his/her neck? Is the color always the same, or do the colors change from time to time? Each season has its own symbolic color, and changing colors is a striking way to signal movement from one season to another.

Some seasons make use of special **SYMBOLS**. Some churches
- use an Advent wreath to mark the four Sundays of Advent,
- cover the cross with a purple veil during Lent, and
- have a procession of palm branches on Palm Sunday.

Does your church use special symbols during any of the seasons?

HOW IT BEGAN

How did we get the Christian Year, anyway? Did some committee of church leaders get together and say, "We should have a Christian Year; let's invent one"? No, it didn't start that way. The Christian Year began and grew because the Church is made up of human beings who are very conscious of **time** and mark important events in their lives by **celebrating**.

GOD RAISED JESUS FROM THE DEAD, and the Church was very happy about that. In fact, the resurrection was SO important that Christians changed their worship day
from Saturday (the Jewish Sabbath)
to Sunday (the day of resurrection). **Every Sunday** they celebrated the resurrection, and when the anniversary of the resurrection came around each year, they had special worship services to give thanks for the resurrection. Because the resurrection had taken place during the Jewish festival of Passover, they called the festival **Pascha** (Passover). Later, they called it **EASTER**.

The original disciples did not expect the resurrection and were not sure what to do when it happened. So Jesus told them to wait in Jerusalem until he sent God's power to them in a special way. During the Jewish harvest festival of Pentecost, the Holy Spirit came upon the disciples and gave them the courage and faith to tell others about Jesus. The Church grew, and every year it celebrated what happened on the Day of **Pentecost**.

So, the Church had TWO FESTIVALS — Easter and Pentecost — and ONE SEASON, the fifty days from Easter to Pentecost.

Then the Church decided that if it was going to celebrate the death and resurrection of Jesus, it should also celebrate his **coming**. So it established the festival of **EPIPHANY**. The word "Epiphany" comes from a Greek word which means **"to show forth."** The festival was set for January 6, and it celebrated everything that God had done to show himself to the world in Jesus Christ

- the birth of Jesus,
- the visit of the Wise Men,
- the baptism of Jesus, and
- Jesus' early miracles.

For the first 300 years of the Church's life, it was illegal to be a Christian. Christians were not allowed to build houses of worship. Sometimes, Roman emperors persecuted Christians because Christians gave their highest allegiance to Christ rather than to the emperor. During those times, worship services had to be held in secret places, and Christians who were caught suffered

- loss of property,
- imprisonment,
- torture,
- exile, and
- death.

Those who suffered and died because of their faith were called **martyrs** (witnesses) and were *remembered* by the Church with special prayers of thanksgiving on the anniversary of their death. Later, other Christians who had set a good example for others were remembered in prayer, too, and the Church began to refer to these anniversaries as **SAINTS' DAYS**.

In the year A.D. 313, the emperor Constantine declared that it was no longer against Roman law to be a Christian. Christians could worship openly. In fact, the emperor helped build houses of worship for them. Now, Christians could worship in public and more celebrations could be held.

In Jerusalem, Christians began to celebrate the events of **HOLY WEEK** by having processions into the city on **Palm Sunday** and out to the Mount of Olives on **Good Friday**.

LENT developed as forty days of special study, fasting, discipline, and prayer for new Christians who were to be baptized on Easter Eve.

Celebrating the birth of Jesus was taken from Epiphany and given its own special season — **CHRISTMAS**.

ADVENT was added as a time of preparation for those who desired to be baptized on Christmas Eve.

So, by the year A.D. 500, the Church had a pretty full calendar, a whole system of *festivals* and *seasons* which helped it prepare for and celebrate **the main events in the life of Jesus**. For over 1,500 years, Christians around the world have used this calendar to help them remember what God has done and to celebrate the gospel.

THE SEASONS OF THE CHRISTIAN YEAR

Even though the seasons of the Christian Year did not develop in the order in which we have them now, it is easier to learn about them if we study them in the order in which they occur in the Christian Year. So, let's look at the seasons in *chronological order* to consider each season's theme, dates, and color and to see how the seasons fit together to tell the story of Jesus.

Advent
Theme: Whenever we know someone important is coming, we make special preparations. We want to be ready. Advent means "coming." It says to us, **"The Christ** (Messiah) **is coming! Get ready!"** It is the season during which we look forward to the coming of Christ at Christmas and prepare our lives to receive him.

It is NOT a time to celebrate Jesus' birth.
It is a time TO GET READY to celebrate his birth.

Dates: Advent begins **four Sundays** before Christmas. Be careful! That is NOT four *weeks* before Christmas, but four *Sundays* before Christmas. Advent begins the Sunday nearest November 30, includes four Sundays, and ends on Christmas Eve.

Very often, the progression of Advent is observed through the use of an **Advent wreath**. The wreath of evergreens symbolizes the eternal life we receive in Christ, and the four candles represent the four Sundays of Advent and help us see the movement of time through the season. Sometimes, these candles are given special names, but their basic purpose is to mark the movement of time toward Christmas.

Color: The liturgical color for Advent is **purple**. In ancient times, purple dye was made from special seashells and was very expensive. Only very wealthy people such as kings could afford purple cloth. Therefore, purple became a symbol of **royalty**. Purple is also a rather **somber** color which reminds us that we need to examine our lives carefully before we join in the celebration of Christmas.

Christmas
Theme: Christmas is the celebration of the INCARNATION. "Carne" is the Latin word for "meat" or "flesh." (It is the same in Spanish.) So, "in-carne" means "in the meat" or "in the flesh." It means that God is NOT sitting way out in space, having nothing to do with us, but that God loves us and has come ALL THE WAY into our lives by taking on human form and being born as a human being. In the birth of Jesus, God is **in-carnate**. So, Christmas says, **"Christ is here! God is with us!"**

Dates: We do not know exactly when Jesus was born. The Bible does not say. The early Christians probably didn't know either. But they were sure of the **fact** that he had been born even if they did not know the exact date it happened.

In the Roman Empire, December 25 was the time of the winter solstice, the shortest day of the year. After that, the days got longer. Therefore, on December 25 pagans celebrated the "birth of the sun." Instead of starting a new holy day, the Church changed the *meaning* of the pagan holiday, celebrating December 25 as the "birth of the *Son*," and calling the festival **Christ-mass**. We have shortened it to **CHRISTMAS**.

Sometimes people argue about whether Jesus was really born on December 25. We don't know. What we DO know is that December 25 was chosen not to celebrate the DATE Jesus was born, but to celebrate the **FACT** that he was born.

However, in biblical times, people did not have clocks to tell them when it was midnight, and it made sense that a new day began when the previous day ended, so days were counted from sundown to sundown rather than from midnight to midnight. That is why, even today, Christmas begins on **Christmas Eve** — after the sun goes down.

Christmas is a **season** as well as a day. It lasts until the festival of Epiphany on January 6. As the song says, there really are twelve days of Christmas.

Color: The liturgical color for Christmas is **white**, the color of purity and light, because Jesus is pure God in the flesh and is the light of the world.

Epiphany
Theme: The ancient Jews believed that the Messiah would come only to them. He would not be concerned with the Gentiles — "the outsiders." But the Wise Men were outsiders, and they were the first to worship Jesus. Also, Jesus preached to and healed foreigners. The apostles took the Good News to the Gentiles and declared that God has no favorites, but loves everyone the same. And that is the message of Epiphany — **"Christ is for everyone."**

Dates: The season begins with the festival of Epiphany on January 6 and continues until the beginning of Lent. The number of days and Sundays in the season depends upon whether Easter and Lent come early or late. There can be as few as four Sundays (if Easter comes early) or as many as nine Sundays (if Easter comes late).

Color: The liturgical color for Epiphany *Day* is **white** because it is a Christ day, showing forth the Messiah. But the color for the remainder of the *season* is **green**, the color of growth, symbolizing the spread of Christ's love to all people.

Lent
Theme: Lent is another season of preparation. It began as a time of special study, fasting, prayer, and discipline for those who wanted to be baptized on Easter Eve. It still is a time of special spiritual preparation for sharing in the death and resurrection of Jesus. Lent says to us, **"Christ will die for you.** Will you be ready to share in his sacrifice?"

Have you ever heard someone say, "I'm giving up cake for Lent"? (It could be soft drinks, movies, or something else.) Since Lent is a time of discipline that looks forward to Jesus' sacrifice, one way to celebrate Lent is to *sacrifice* something of value during that time.

But discipline does not have to be giving up something. It can also be *adding on* something — like visiting sick people, writing to friends, or making up with enemies.

Dates: Lent begins forty days before Easter, NOT COUNTING SUNDAYS. Sundays are not included because Sundays are always festivals of the resurrection, "little Easters." Therefore, they do not fit into a time of fasting. (How can you feast and fast at the same time?) The first day of Lent is called **Ash Wednesday**. Its name comes from the practice of marking the foreheads of penitent worshipers with a cross of ashes obtained by burning the palm branches from the previous Palm Sunday. Lent ends on Easter Eve.

Color: The liturgical color for Lent is **purple**, that somber, royal color. Both Advent and Lent use purple because they are seasons of preparation.

Easter
Theme: Easter was the first festival of the Church. It is a celebration of the resurrection of Jesus. It says, "**Christ is risen!** He is risen indeed. Hallelujah!" All people are invited to share in his victory over sin and death.

In the early Church, the festival was called **Pascha**, which comes from the Jewish word for "Passover," because the resurrection took place during the feast of Passover. But when Christian missionaries reached northern Europe, they found Teutonic people celebrating a spring festival of new birth named after their goddess of spring, **Eastre**. Because the two festivals came about the same time of year and because Christians began celebrating spring with their neighbors, Christians gradually began calling their festival **Easter**. Even in our culture today, many people get the two festivals confused and think that Easter has more to do with flowers, rabbits, colored eggs, and new clothes than with the resurrection of our Lord.

Dates: For a long time, Christians argued about when Easter should be celebrated. The church in **eastern Europe** said it should come during the time of the Jewish Passover. But the Jewish calendar is based on cycles of the moon rather than cycles of the sun, so Passover can come any time during the week. Therefore, Good Friday could come on Tuesday and Easter could come on Thursday. The church in **western Europe** said Good Friday should always be on Friday and Easter should always be on Sunday.

In the year A.D. 325, they reached a **compromise**. A Church council decided that Easter would be celebrated on
- the first Sunday
- after the first full moon
- after spring begins.

That means that Easter can come as early as March 22 or as late as April 25.

The date of Easter effects most of the rest of the Christian Year, because both Lent and Pentecost are tied to Easter. Lent comes forty days BEFORE Easter (not counting Sundays) and

Pentecost comes fifty days AFTER Easter. So, when the date of Easter changes, the dates for Lent and Pentecost change, too.

> IF EASTER COMES EARLIER,
> Lent and Pentecost come earlier,
> Epiphany is shorter, and
> Pentecost is longer.

> IF EASTER COMES LATER,
> Lent and Pentecost come later,
> Epiphany is longer, and
> Pentecost is shorter.

Easter is a festival, but it also is a **season**. It begins on Easter Eve and continues until Pentecost — **fifty days** later. So the season of Easter includes Easter Day plus six other Sundays.

Colors: Because Easter is a Christ festival of victory, the liturgical color for Easter is white, the color for victory, purity, and light.

Pentecost

Theme: "Pente" is the Greek word for "five" and "Pentekonta" is the Greek word for **fifty**, so the Jewish festival which came **fifty** days after the Passover was called **Pentecost**. It was during this festival that Christ sent the Holy Spirit upon the early disciples to give them power and courage to spread the message of Jesus. Therefore, the message of Pentecost is, **"Christ has sent the Holy Spirit** upon the Church so that it can carry the message of God's love to the ends of the earth."

Dates: Pentecost begins fifty days after Easter and continues until the beginning of Advent (or until the last Sunday of August if your church celebrates Kingdomtide).

Trinity Sunday is the first Sunday after Pentecost. In some churches, the season is called **Trinity** rather than Pentecost.

MODERN CHANGES IN THE CHRISTIAN YEAR

The Christian Year has developed over a long period of time. That development is still taking place.

Since the early 1960s, some denominations have been making changes in the Christian Year. Other denominations have accepted some, or all, or none of these changes. So do not be surprised if what you do in your church is not exactly the same as what is done in other churches.

METHODISTS made one of the changes. Some Methodists said, "The Christian Year is incomplete. The end of history is not the sending of the Holy Spirit on the Church. The end of history is the **Kingdom of God**. Why don't we have a season which celebrates Christ as King?" Others said, "The season of Pentecost is too long. For six months, the theme remains the same, and the color remains the same. It gets boring. It would be better to have two seasons during this time."

So, in 1964, The Methodist Church put these two ideas together and created the season of **KINGDOMTIDE**. The season BEGAN on the last Sunday of August and continued until Advent. Its THEME was **"Christ is King!"** The COLOR was green, the color of growth, to show that God wants all people to be included in the Kingdom of God.

But, because not all Methodists celebrated the season, and because other denominations did not include it in their Christian Year, in 1992, The United Methodist Church dropped the SEASON, but kept the NAME. Now the Sundays after Pentecost are called "Season After Pentecost (or Kingdomtide)," and the last Sunday of the season is the Festival of Christ the King.

But, because some United Methodist pastors *liked* the new season and were not required to drop it, some United Methodists still celebrate KINGDOMTIDE while others do not. You will need to ask your pastor **what** he does and **why**.

The **ROMAN CATHOLIC CHURCH** made another change. Vatican Council II (1962-1964) authorized a new lectionary for the Roman Catholic Church. By the mid-1970s, some other denominations began to use it and to revise it. This lectionary divides the Christian Year into **TWO CYCLES** — the Christmas Cycle (Advent, Christmas, and Epiphany Day) and the Easter Cycle (Lent, Easter, and Pentecost Day). There is no Epiphany *Season* or Pentecost *Season*. The Sundays following these two special festivals are called "Ordinary Time." "Ordinary" means "common," "unexceptional," or "not special." Therefore these Sundays are not included in the other seasons and do not have a special theme.

Some pastors like this pattern of two cycles because 1) it fits the American custom of emphasizing Christmas and Easter more than the other seasons and because 2) "ordinary time" gives pastors an opportunity to "do their own thing" for part of the year.

Other pastors believe that 1) all the seasons are important in the Christ story, and 2) that every day of the Christian Year should be related to some part of the story of Jesus.

Therefore, some churches, such as the Episcopal Church and the Presbyterian Church have stayed with the year of six seasons. The United Methodist Church has tried to give pastors options by recognizing the two cycles but calling these two seasons "Season After the Epiphany (Ordinary Time)" and "Season After Pentecost (Ordinary Time or Kingdomtide)."

Because all denominations and all pastors are not observing the Christian Year in exactly the same way, you will need to ask your pastor **what** your church does and **why** you do it that way.

THE STORY OF JESUS

In spite of these changes, the PURPOSE of the Christian Year remains the same — to celebrate the story of Jesus from the announcement of his coming to the Kingdom of God. We celebrate the whole story as we move through the year.

ADVENT — Christ is coming!
CHRISTMAS — Christ is here!
EPIPHANY — Christ is for everyone!
LENT — Christ will suffer and die!
EASTER — Christ is risen!
PENTECOST — Christ sends the Holy Spirit!
KINGDOMTIDE — Christ is King!

(I included Kingdomtide because I think it completes the story in a meaningful way.)

HOW MUCH DO YOU REMEMBER?

True or False

T	F	The Christian Year is based on major events in the history of Methodism.
T	F	A lectionary is a list of Bible readings.
T	F	The season which prepares for the coming of Christ is Advent.
T	F	Scripture, prayers, and hymns can express the theme of a season.
T	F	The two seasons which use white are Epiphany and Lent.
T	F	Easter is the first Sunday after the first full moon of spring.
T	F	Lent begins fifty days before Easter.
T	F	The coming of the Wise Men is remembered during Epiphany.
T	F	Pentecost celebrates the birth of Jesus.
T	F	The Christian Year never changes.

Correctly match the items in the left column with items in the right column.

Advent	Begins January 6
Lent	The first festival of the church
Christmas	The disciples receive power and faith
Kingdomtide	A season of twelve days
Pentecost	"Let Christ control your life."
Easter	A wreath and four candles
Epiphany	Does not include Sundays

What Worship Is

Worship is the most important thing we do.
Worship is the most important action of a Christian congregation.
Worship is the scene of most of an acolyte's service.

Therefore, even though you might know how to light candles, carry a banner, or help the pastor with Holy Baptism, unless you know the **meaning** of worship and **understand** what is going on in the worship service, you will not really appreciate your service as an acolyte. So, let's learn something about worship.

Everyone worships. That is a very broad statement, but it is true. Everyone does not worship the same thing. Not everyone worships the God who is revealed in Jesus Christ. But EVERYONE worships SOMETHING.

Our word **worship** comes from an old Anglo-Saxon word — **woerthan** (pronounced "were-THAWN"). Woerthan had two meanings. The *first* was "to declare how much something is worth." In English, it was written "worth-ship." But worth-ship is hard to say. (Just try saying it rapidly about five times!) So, "th" and the hyphen were dropped, and the word became **worship**.

The original meaning is still there, though. Worship means TO DECLARE HOW MUCH SOMETHING IS WORTH. Worship has to do with values, and all of us live by values.

Some things are important.
Some things are less important.
Some things are VERY important (Wow!)
Some things are ... yuk!
Some thing is MOST important — at the TOP!

Whatever is at the TOP,
      Whatever is MOST important,
            Whatever is WORTH THE MOST,
                  THAT is what a person **WORSHIPS**.
                    For that person, THAT is **GOD**.

It might be

- popularity,
- success,
- fun,
- power,
- money,
- comfort,
- fame,
- "things,"
- nature, or
- animals.

Or it might be the God who created the universe and sent Jesus to show us that God loves us.

But EVERYONE has SOMETHING at the top. Everyone has a god (small "g"). Everyone worships something.

NOTE: Christians believe that the God who created the universe and whose love is revealed in Jesus Christ is the only god who is REALLY God, so we use a capital "G." Anything which is treated like a god but is not really God is an *idol*.

But that is not all! Woerthan has a **second** meaning. Not only did it mean "to declare how much something is worth," but it also means "to be." That may seem strange until we stop to think that what is most important to us REALLY DOES determine the kind of person we become. It works like this —

What is most important to us determines our goals.
To reach those goals, we shape our lives in certain ways.
How we shape our lives determines the person we become.

As Paul Rayner said, "What a person is, or what a person becomes, depends on what a person worships." That is why

WORSHIP IS THE MOST IMPORTANT THING WE DO.

WORSHIP IS ACTION

Usually, we think of worship as something we "attend." It is like going to a play or a movie. We get dressed up, go to the church building, and watch the worship leaders (pastor, acolytes, liturgist, choir, etc.) "do their thing." Then we go home. We say that we have "been to church" or that we have "attended" church.

That is not the way early Christians looked at it. The New Testament was written in GREEK, and the Greek words which we translate into English as "worship" are VERBS. They are ACTION words. They indicate that worship is not something we "attend," but something we DO.

The *first* Greek word is **SEBOMAI** (pronounced "SEB-ah-my"). It means **"to lift up high"** or **"to exalt."** It means we recognize that
God is the HIGHEST
God is the GREATEST
God is at the TOP
GOD IS #1.

And we stand in God's presence with reverence and awe to give
God the glory and honor and love which God deserves.
We PRAISE God.

28

The *second* Greek word is **PROSKUNEO** (pronounced "pros-kew-NEH-oh"). I means **"to bow down."** In biblical times, whenever a person came into the presence of the king, he would BOW DOWN with his hands, knees, and forehead on the ground. Sometimes, he would kiss the king's feet. (Literally, proskuneo means "to kiss forward.") In this position, he was completely helpless and completely under the control of the king. So "bowing down" was a way of showing complete subservience and obedience to the king.

Today in worship, we BOW DOWN
to show that God is our king,
to show humility in God's presence,
to admit that we need God's love,
and
to find out what God wants us to do.

It is not very often that we bow completely down with our hands, knees, and head on the floor the way our Muslim neighbors pray. Sometimes we simply bow our heads. Other times, we kneel on our knees. But, the meaning is still the same — God is King and we are God's people.

The *third* Greek word is **LATREUO** (pronounced "lah-TRUE-oh"). It means **"to serve."** Whenever the king told a person to do something, the person was expected to do it. Disobedience to the king was a VERY serious offense that could lead to punishment by death.

Today, LATREUO reminds us that even though our worship of God might BEGIN in the house of worship, it DOES NOT END there. The love, mercy, and forgiveness that we receive in worship are to be passed on to every person we meet.

THESE THREE WORDS GO TOGETHER.

What we lift up as number one (sebomai)
is
what we bow down to (proskuneo)
and
what we serve with our lives (latreuo).

AND ALL OF THEM POINT TO GOD.
God is the one we praise.
God is the one before whom we bow.
God is the one who speaks to us.
God is the one we serve.

The center of attention in worship is GOD!

In worship, we **ACT OUT** our worship in various ways. One way is through WORDS.
We can express SEBOMAI by saying, "God is the greatest."
We can express PROSKUNEO by saying, "Lord, have mercy on me."
We can express LATREUO by saying, "Here I am, Lord; send me."

Pay attention to the words of the call to worship, the prayers, the hymns, and the other acts of worship, and you will discover that these WORDS have been written and chosen to help us act out our worship.

Another way to act out our worship is through **POSTURE** (body position). In our culture, we **STAND** to show honor and respect. We stand to pledge allegiance to the flag, and we stand and clap to show gratitude for a concert. It is hard to lift something very high or to express how great something is while sitting down. Therefore, the posture for praise (**sebomai**) and thanksgiving is to STAND.

Standing is also the posture for serving (**latreuo**). It is a posture which says, "I am here and ready to go to work!" So we stand when we present our gifts or offer ourselves in service to God.

On the other hand, it is very difficult to act out **proskuneo** (bowing down) while standing. How can you be down when you are up? It doesn't work. Sitting with the **HEAD BOWED** is better. (At least, you are part way down.) But bowing with the whole body — **KNEELING** — is better. That is why many Christians kneel for prayers (especially prayers of confession), for Holy Communion, or whenever they pass in front of the altar.

The third posture used in worship is **SITTING**. It does not fit directly with any of the New Testament words for worship, but it is a very practical posture for the longer portions of the service which do not call for standing or kneeling. (It would be very tiring to stand or kneel throughout the sermon.) So, sitting is the traditional posture for acts of worship involving instruction.

Down through the centuries, the Church has developed a simple rule for the posture of worship:
- STAND for praise, thanks, and special acts of honor.
- KNEEL for confession and prayers (except praise).
- SIT for instruction.

NOTE: It might be fun for your pastor to lead you in some *"acolyte calisthenics."* As the pastor calls out the words "sebomai, proskuneo, latreuo, and instruction," you stand, kneel, or sit to show the proper posture for that type of worship.

CONGREGATIONAL WORSHIP

Some people ask,
"Why is it necessary to worship with other people?"
"Why can't I worship by myself in my own way?"
"Why does the church keep urging me to worship with the congregation?"

The New Testament word for CHURCH means "those who are called out." The word CONGREGATION means "those who are gathered together." **We are not Christian all by ourselves.** We are Christian along with others who follow Christ. We are part of the **family of God.** So we worship together. It is one way of saying to ourselves, to each other, and to the world that we are bound to each other by faith in Christ.

This does not mean that you cannot worship alone. You can, and you should. But not all the time. Private devotions are not meant to *replace* congregational worship but to ADD to it. You should do BOTH.

The person who worships alone *all the time* will soon face three problems:
1. Worship will become careless and hurried.
2. Worship will become incomplete (usually omitting praise and confession).
3. Worship will be crowded out by other activities.

The person who stops hearing the scriptures in church
> soon stops reading the Bible at home.

The person who stops praying with the congregation
> soon stops praying at home.

The person who stops being part of the people of God
> soon drops out of doing Christ's work.

CONGREGATIONAL WORSHIP IS NECESSARY FOR A STRONG AND VITAL FAITH.

"But, is once a week really necessary?" All of us have asked that question at some time. But is it the right question? Maybe we should ask

*   "How often do I need to remember that God (not me) is number one?"
*   "How often do I need to be forgiven for doing wrong?"
*   "How often do I need God's help?"
*   "How often do I need to hear what God wants me to do?"

If we look at it this way, surely once a week is not too often. It may not be enough. That is why weekly worship with the congregation PLUS daily private worship is a good combination.

"But, why do we have to go to church? Can't we worship anywhere?" Of course you *can* worship anywhere. God is not limited to a special place. But, sometimes we FORGET to worship in other places.

A person CAN worship on the golf course, but usually she doesn't.
> (She is more interested in hitting the ball than in worshiping God.)

A person CAN worship while fishing, but usually he doesn't.
> (He is more interested in catching fish than in worshiping God.)

A person CAN worship while hiking in the mountains, but often that worship is incomplete.
> (We remember God the creator, but forget God the savior.)

Besides, SURROUNDINGS AFFECT WHAT WE DO.

You *can* study geography in a bare room, but having maps, charts, and pictures HELPS.

You *can* paint a picture of the ocean while miles away from the ocean, but being on the beach HELPS.

You *can* worship God without symbols, organ, and hymnals, but having them HELPS.

We do not have houses of worship because we cannot worship without them. WE HAVE HOUSES OF WORSHIP BECAUSE THEY **HELP** US WORSHIP GOD by
- giving us a place to gather for worship and
- surrounding us with things that HELP us worship.

THE ACOLYTE IN WORSHIP

All of this talk about worship has serious implications for acolytes and how they serve. What you do to LEAD worship needs to fit with what worship IS.

Because God is the center of attention in worship, be sure that the way you walk, sit, and carry out your duties does not make people think about *you* instead of God.

Because worship is something people DO rather than "attend," you should remember that you are NOT a performer putting on a show, but a WORSHIP LEADER who is there to help others worship.

Because you have come to worship too, be sure that you participate in the entire service and not just the parts you lead.

Because you have come to worship and serve God, be sure to do your VERY BEST.

HOW MUCH DO YOU REMEMBER?

True or False

T	F	Only Christians, Buddhists, and Mormons worship.
T	F	Every person has values to live by.
T	F	Whatever is most important to a person is his/her god.
T	F	All people worship the God revealed in Jesus Christ.
T	F	What we worship determines the kind of person we become.
T	F	Worship is a program we watch.
T	F	Sebomai means "to serve."
T	F	The Greek New Testament has more than one word for "worship."

Multiple Choice (check the best answer)

1. Worship is concerned mainly with
____ a. printed songs.
____ b. how much things are worth.
____ c. listening to a sermon.

2. Sebomai can be translated as
____ a. "praise."
____ b. "I am number one."
____ c. "Get down on your knees."

3. Posture refers to
____ a. singing in a loud voice.
____ b. body positions.
____ c. the sanctuary.

4. The usual posture for praise is
____ a. sitting.
____ b. kneeling.
____ c. standing.

5. Christians worship with the congregation because
____ a. they are part of God's family.
____ b. God will hate them if they don't.
____ c. it is the only possible way to worship.

Ritual And Liturgy

Two words used very often in the discussion of worship are **ritual** and **liturgy**. Sometimes people speak as if they are the same. They are similar, but not the same.

A **RITUAL** is a set way of doing something. Any person or group which has decided upon a set way of doing something has a ritual.

>Families have rituals for getting out of bed, eating breakfast, and getting off to work or school.

>Schools have rituals for beginning class each day.

>There are rituals for scout meetings, football games, military parades, the dedication of public buildings, and many other events.

Rituals are NECESSARY if a number of people are going to do something TOGETHER without chaos.

>IMAGINE trying to start a football game when each coach wants to warm up first, there is no way to decide who will kick off, and the band directors want to march on the field while both teams are warming up.

>IMAGINE the dedication of a public building where the mayor wants to cut the ribbon before anyone arrives, the choir wants to sing while the mayor is talking, and the minister wants to pronounce the benediction before the service is over.

>IMAGINE 150 people trying to worship together when some want to sing while others pray and others are taking up the offering.

>CHAOS!

Rituals allow us to do things TOGETHER with some kind of order.

A **LITURGY** is a *special kind* of ritual. That means that every liturgy is a ritual, but not every ritual is a liturgy. Does that sound confusing? Then think about this:

Every apple is a fruit, but every fruit is not an apple.
(Oranges and bananas are fruits, too.)

Every human being is an animal, but every animal is not a human being.
(Dogs and cats are animals, too.)

Every liturgy is a ritual, but every ritual is not a liturgy.
(There are other kinds of rituals, too.)

LITURGY comes from another Greek word which can be translated "worship." The word is **leitourgia**. When you change the Greek letters into English letters, it comes out like this:

```
λ  ε  ι  τ  ο  υ  ρ  γ  ι  α
l  e  i  t  o  u  r  g  i  a
l     i  t     u  r  g  y
```

Literally, it means **"the work of the people."** In some ancient literature, it refers to the volunteer service people gave to help the community be a better place to live. In the New Testament, it refers to what people do together when they come to worship God. In modern usage,

A LITURGY IS A RITUAL IN WHICH **EVERYONE** PARTICIPATES.

If the ritual is performed by someone else and you just watch, it is *not* a liturgy. If the ritual is one in which EVERYONE takes part, it *is* a liturgy.

LITURGICAL AND NON-LITURGICAL WORSHIP

Some churches **require** that a certain liturgy be used for worship. They have developed the liturgy over a long period of time and find that it provides the kind of worship experience they want. So, they **require** the pastor to use that liturgy for worship, and the pastor can get into trouble if that liturgy is not used. We call these churches LITURGICAL CHURCHES. That does not mean that these are the only churches which *have* a liturgy, but that they are the churches which *require* that a certain liturgy be used. The major liturgical churches in the United States are the Roman Catholic Church, the Episcopal Church, the Lutheran Church, and the Orthodox Churches.

Other churches *do not require* a certain liturgy be used, but provide a liturgy which is RECOMMENDED to the churches. It is hoped that the liturgy will be used, but the pastor will not be in trouble if it is not used. Some of these churches are the United Church of Christ, the United Methodist Church, the United Presbyterian Church, and the Christian Church (Disciples of Christ).

Still other churches feel that a liturgy is too formal and rigid and does not allow enough individual freedom in worship. Therefore, they are *opposed* to an established liturgy. The pastor is expected to develop an order of worship which is satisfactory to the pastor and the congregation. The pastor is also free to change the order of worship whenever he/she desires and the congregation does not object. Very often, these churches refer to themselves as FREE CHURCHES because they are free to choose whatever order of service they like. Some of the churches which follow this practice are the Baptist Churches, the Pentecostal Churches, the Nazarene Church, and the Assembly of God.

BUT CHURCHES CHANGE. Because of history, the needs of people, or even geography, churches may change their ways of worship.

FOR EXAMPLE, the United Methodist Church came out of The Church of England, which is a very formal liturgical church. John Wesley recommended that Methodists in this country follow the Church of England liturgy.

35

BUT, how could Methodist circuit riders carry robes, banners, candles, crosses, and prayer books on their horses as they rode from town to town? They didn't even have churches to meet in. As a result, Methodist worship became very informal and Holy Communion was celebrated only when the preacher was there.

Today, most United Methodists live in towns and cities and have pastors who serve them for longer periods of time. Therefore, many United Methodist worship services are becoming more liturgical and Holy Communion is celebrated more often.

ADVANTAGES AND DISADVANTAGES

As with most things in life, there are both advantages and disadvantages to having a liturgy or not having one. I will simply list some of them so that you can discuss them with your pastor.

Some Advantages Of Using A Liturgy
1. Because most liturgies have a long history, the liturgy can help connect us to the church of the past and the church of the future.
2. Many liturgies are used over a large geographical area, and people can feel at home in worship even in a strange place.
3. The liturgy provides a familiar outline for worship, yet also provides for a variety of acts of worship within that outline.
4. Usually, the liturgy is built around the Christian Year and helps the congregation celebrate the whole gospel as it moves through the year.
5. Most of the content of the liturgy is from the Bible, so we learn the Bible message by participating in worship.
6. Usually, the service is dignified and reverent.
7. The entire congregation participates in the acts of worship.

Some Possible Problems With Using A Liturgy
1. Unless the liturgy is used wisely, the service may become rigid and mechanical.
2. Sometimes the liturgy can become very FORMAL. (That means that the *way* something is done is more important than *doing it*.)
3. The liturgy may be confusing to newcomers who are expected to participate in the worship service but do not know what to do.
4. The liturgy may be so old that its language and actions are out-of-date and are not meaningful to the worshipers.

Some Advantages Of NOT Using A Liturgy
1. The worship service can be varied to satisfy the likes and dislikes of the pastor and the congregation.
2. The entire service can be centered around a theme of the pastor's choosing.
3. The service may be very informal and allow for more individual expression.
4. If there is not a great deal of congregational participation, newcomers find it easy to follow the order of service.

Some Possible Problems With NOT Using A Liturgy

1. There is a tendency for worship to become something we "attend" or watch rather than something we DO.
2. The worship service may be determined by the whims and prejudices of the pastor and congregation rather than by the biblical meaning of worship.
3. The service may become so "informal" that it loses its dignity and reverence.
4. People may not know what to expect when worshiping in a particular church for the first time.
5. The service may not have much historical meaning.
6. Only a few festivals and seasons of the Christian Year might be celebrated while others are ignored.

MORE THAN ONE POSSIBILITY

Worship is the most important thing we do, and in a world of rapid transportation and communication, it is important that Christians understand one another and be able to worship together. IT WILL BE A GREAT DAY when Christians *stop criticizing* and ridiculing one another because they worship differently and we *begin to understand* and learn from each other.

> It is NOT NECESSARY that ALL Christians worship the same way.
> Different **cultures** and **nations** develop different ways to express themselves.
> Different **histories** cause people to develop different customs and habits.
> Different **people** have different needs, desires, likes, and dislikes.

So, we do NOT all have to fit into the same mold.
We do NOT all have to worship the same way.

BUT HOW DO WE DECIDE?

Let me suggest FIVE GUIDELINES and FOUR QUESTIONS that might help.

FIRST, study your own church tradition to find out WHAT you are doing and WHY you are doing it.

SECOND, discover HOW other Christians worship and WHY they worship that way.

THIRD, take very seriously the advantages and disadvantages of having a liturgy or not having a liturgy.

FOURTH, remember the Greek words which the New Testament uses for worship:
- sebomai,
- proskuneo,
- latreuo, and
- leitourgia.

37

Then, ASK YOURSELF THESE QUESTIONS:

1. Does our worship **lift up** God as the greatest and most important?

2. Does our worship lead us to **bow down** before God to receive God's love and to hear what God says to us?

3. Does our worship lead us out into the world to **serve** God in everything we do?

4. Is our worship something we all **do together**, rather than a "program" for the congregation to watch?

Following these guidelines and answering these questions will help you know **why** you worship the way you do and help you **appreciate** other Christians who worship in a different way.

HOW MUCH DO YOU REMEMBER?

True or False

T	F	Ritual and liturgy are exactly the same.
T	F	Every liturgy is a ritual.
T	F	Every ritual is a liturgy.
T	F	A liturgy is a ritual in which everyone participates.
T	F	All churches require the pastor to use a certain liturgy.
T	F	"Free churches" have no problems with worship.
T	F	"Liturgy" comes from a French word which means "boring."
T	F	The United Methodist Church recommends a liturgy but does not require that it be used.
T	F	All true Christians should worship in the same way.

The Order Of Worship

Now that you know something about worship, ritual, and liturgy, we need to apply that knowledge to the ORDER OF WORSHIP.

Sometimes, people refer to it as the "program," but we have seen that worship is not a program we attend but something we DO to declare how much God is worth. So "order of worship" is a better term to use. The order of worship does two things:

1. It lists the "order" in which acts of worship come, so that we know the SERMON will come after the CALL TO WORSHIP and the BENEDICTION will come toward the end.

2. It helps the congregation worship together in an "orderly" way without confusion.

If your church **requires** that a certain liturgy be used or **recommends** that a certain order of worship be followed, it probably will be printed in the front or the back of
*   The Book of Prayer,
*   The Book of Worship, or
*   The Hymnal.

In the United Methodist Church, the order of worship is found in the front of *The United Methodist Hymnal*, starting on page 2. In fact, this hymnal includes
*   the basic pattern of worship (an outline),
*   a complete order of worship including acts of worship and instructions,
*   and three orders for the celebration of Holy Communion.

If your denomination provides an order of worship, where is it found? (If you don't know, ask your pastor.)

If your denomination *does NOT provide* an order of worship,
or
if your pastor *does not follow* the recommended order,
ask your pastor for an outline of the order of worship which is used on Sunday morning.

Orders of worship provided by the denomination usually include instructions which tell the pastor and people what to do. These instructions are called RUBRICS. When prayer books were printed by hand, these instructions were printed in red ink. Since some red ink was made from red earth and the Latin word for "red earth" is *rubrica*, the instructions printed in red were called *rubrics*.

Today, some books have the rubrics printed in red, while in others, they are printed in *italics*. HOW ARE YOUR INSTRUCTIONS PRINTED?

If you read carefully, you will notice that there are THREE KINDS of rubrics.

One is a mild command which says,
*   "A prayer of thanksgiving **is** offered."
*   "All pray the Lord's Prayer."

Another is a stronger command which says,
- "Two or three Scripture readings **should** be used."

The third is a suggestion which says,
- "Responses **may** include one of the following."
- "A hymn, psalm, or anthem **may** be sung."

The rubrics which say "may" give the pastor a great deal of freedom, even if the liturgy is required. But pastors use this freedom with great care so that they make only those changes which will make the worship service more meaningful.

ACTS OF WORSHIP

A service of worship consists of a variety of ACTS of worship which help us declare how much God is worth. Exactly which acts of worship are included and the order in which they come may vary from one service to another.

The following acts of worship are used by many churches, though some may be called by different names. You do not need to memorize these definitions (unless your pastor requires that), but you should be able to state accurately IN YOUR OWN WORDS what each act of worship IS and WHY it is in the service of worship. (A good exercise is to try to match each act of worship with one of the Greek words for "worship.")

Prelude	Introductory music which helps us think about God and prepare for meaningful worship.
Scripture Sentences Call To Worship Introit	Brief passages from the Bible which invite us to worship. ("Introit" is pronounced "IN-trow-it" and means "words for entering.")
Greeting	Greeting the people *in the name of Christ* (not just saying, "Good morning.")
Hymn	A poem of praise set to music, usually sung by the congregation.
Invocation Opening Prayer	A prayer which asks God to be present. (The Latin word "invocare" means "to call upon.")
Confession Of Sin	A prayer by the congregation which admits that we have done wrong and need to be forgiven.
Act Of Pardon	A statement, often from the Scriptures, which assures us that through Christ our sin is forgiven.
The Lord's Prayer	The prayer Jesus taught his disciples.

The Psalter	A selection of Hebrew hymns from the book of Psalms used as a congregational act of praise.
Gloria Patri	A short hymn of praise to the Trinity which takes its name from the Latin words for "Glory be to the Father."
Anthem	A sacred composition, often with words from the Scriptures, usually sung by the choir.
Scripture Lessons	Readings from different parts of the Bible. OLD TESTAMENT lessons tell us about how God worked through the lives of the Hebrew people. NEW TESTAMENT lessons tell us who Jesus was, what he did, and why we should follow him. GOSPEL means "good news." The Gospels are the first four books of the New Testament. EPISTLE means "letter." The Epistles are letters written by Saint Paul and other early Christians which are included in the New Testament.
Confession Of Faith Affirmation Of Faith Creed	A Christian "pledge of allegiance" through which we declare what we believe. ("Creed" comes from the Latin word "credo" which means "I believe.")
Doxology	A short hymn of praise which takes its name from "doxa," the Greek word for "praise."
Collect	A brief prayer which "collects" our thoughts and focuses them on an idea or theme. (Accent the FIRST syllable.)
Concerns And Prayers	The sharing of joys and concerns of the congregation that are to be lifted up in prayer.
Pastoral Prayer	A prayer by the pastor which lifts up the needs of the congregation and the world.
Offertory	The giving of our gifts and our lives to God in faithful service.
Sermon	A spoken message by the pastor (or layperson) which explains a passage of Scripture and applies it to our daily lives.
Invitation	An invitation to follow Christ in some special way, such as accepting Christ as Lord, joining the church, or doing some special work for Christ.
Benediction	A blessing which says God wants good things to happen to the people. Often spoken as people prepare to leave.

Postlude	The concluding music of the service which provides time for silent prayer and meditation before leaving.
Amen	The Hebrew word for "truly" or "it is true." It is used to show that the worshiper agrees with what has been said or sung.
Hallelujah	A Hebrew word which means "praise the Lord." "Alleluia" is the Greek form. (Greek has no "h" or "j.")

MORE ACTS OF WORSHIP

Some churches include other acts of worship. Even if they are not included in the order of worship you use, it is a good idea to know about them in case you worship in a different congregation.

Verses and Responses	Short sentences, usually from the Scriptures, which mark movement from one major part of the service to another.
Gloria In Excelsis	A hymn of praise which means (in Latin) "Glory be to God on high."
Sanctus	A brief hymn of praise which receives its name from the Latin word for "holy."
Agnus Dei	A hymn which asks Christ to have mercy on us and grant us peace. In Latin, "Angus Dei" (pronounced "on-yoos day-ee") means "Lamb of God," a name used for Jesus.
Chant	A song which uses a very simple melody and very few notes to provide a way to talk to music.
Canticle	An ancient hymn, usually with words from the Scriptures.
Litany	A prayer which the worship leader and the congregation pray responsively.

Now, it is time for you to STUDY the order of worship your church uses. Find out
- WHAT acts of worship are included.
- WHY these are included and others are left out.
- WHY they come in the order they do.
- WHAT each act is intended to do.
- WHAT the pastor wants the service to accomplish.
- HOW your service adds meaning to worship.

IF YOU UNDERSTAND ALL OF THIS, YOU WILL BE A VERY EFFECTIVE WORSHIP LEADER.

HOW MUCH DO YOU REMEMBER?

True or False

T   F   All churches use the same order of worship.

T   F   Most orders of service can be found in the back of the Bible.

T   F   Rubrics are instructions for worship.

T   F   The prelude is music played to cover up noise.

T   F   "Doxology" gets its name from the Greek word for "praise."

T   F   The benediction is a spoken blessing.

T   F   "Amen" is a Hebrew word which means "it is true."

T   F   The Lord's Prayer was used before Jesus was born.

T   F   An "Order of Worship" tells the order for doing acts of worship.

T   F   A hymn is a poem set to music.

Match the following words with their proper description.

Hymn   A sacred composition sung by the choir.

Psalter   A statement of what we believe.

Invocation   A blessing that says God wants good things to happen to us.

Sermon   A prayer which asks God to be present.

Anthem   A song of praise, usually sung by the congregation.

Creed   A spoken message which explains a passage of Scripture and applies it to our daily lives.

Benediction   A selection of Hebrew hymns from the book of Psalms.

The Sacraments

Sacraments are special acts of worship which ACT OUT God's love in our lives. Sacraments are DRAMAS which use symbols to show us God's love.

In the Bible, we **read** about what God did for us in Christ.
In a sermon, we **hear** what God did for us in Christ.
In a sacrament, we **ACT OUT** what God did for us in Christ.

Protestant Christians believe that for a service to be called a sacrament it must meet two conditions:
1. It must use a symbol to act out God's love.
2. It must be an act which Jesus told the Church to use.

Since only two services meet BOTH of those requirements, Protestant Christians say that there are only two sacraments —
- HOLY BAPTISM and
- HOLY COMMUNION.

The Roman Catholic Church lists five other services as sacraments: confirmation, penance, marriage, ordination, and unction. Protestants believe that these are very important sacred rites. But, because SOME do not use a symbol to act out God's love and NONE was commanded by Jesus, they do not count them as sacraments.

It is traditional to talk about three parts of a sacrament.

Promise   A statement that God loves us even when we do not deserve it and will forgive our sin if we admit that we need to be forgiven.

Symbol   A physical object which is used to dramatize the promise.

Faith   Trust that God will keep the promise.

In a sacrament,
- the liturgy communicates God's promise,
- a symbol illustrates that promise, and
- celebrating the sacrament shows that we trust God.

Sometimes, we speak of the sacraments as MEANS OF GRACE. They are **channels** through which God's **grace** comes to us.

BUT WHAT IS GRACE?

To understand the meaning of grace, we need to understand the meaning of another word — SIN.

The Bible teaches that human beings have been created in the **image of God**. That is a picture-language way of saying that not only have we been created BY God, but also we have been created FOR God. God has created us in such a way that we can
- know God,
- get along with God,
- worship God,
- love God, and
- obey God.

God CAN BE the most important thing in our lives. God CAN BE the center of our lives. God CAN BE at the top. God CAN BE number one.

But is that the way we live? Hardly! Instead of saying, "Yes, God, you are most important," we say,

> "No! **I** am most important!
> **I** am number one!
> **I** will run my own life.
> I don't need God to tell **me** what to do!"

In this way, we turn our backs on God, run away from God, and follow our own foolish ways. That is what the Bible calls SIN.

And what does God say to us? God says,
- "I love you, anyway."
- "You are foolish, but I love you."
- "You are rebellious, but I love you."
- "You are sinful, but I love you."
- "You don't deserve it, but I love you."
- "I love you **in spite of** your sin."

THAT IS **GRACE**
- love which loves us in spite of our sin.
- love which forgives our sin.
- love which we *cannot* earn or deserve.
- love which we *do not need* to earn or deserve.
- love which comes as a FREE GIFT.

Literally, the word "grace" means **"a free gift."** So, when we say that the sacraments are MEANS OF GRACE, we are saying that the sacraments are special acts of worship which act out the FREE GIFT of God's love in our lives.

THE SACRAMENT OF HOLY BAPTISM

The **PROMISE** of Holy Baptism is that
- God loves you,
- will always love you, and
- will never stop loving you.

45

It is the promise of GRACE. It is the promise that even though you have turned away from God and tried to be free of God's control, God has not turned away from you and will never turn away from you. God still loves you, will forgive your sin, and will give you another chance. Wow!

BUT HOW CAN WE BE SURE?
        It is such a fantastic promise!
        It is almost more than a person can believe!
        How can we be sure?
        Is there any EVIDENCE?

Yes, there is evidence, and the name of that evidence is "JESUS." Jesus spent all his life loving people who "did not deserve it," people who were outcasts of his society — fishermen, tax collectors, harlots, lepers, cripples, people who broke the laws of religion.

This got him into trouble with the religious authorities who believed that sinners should be scorned rather than loved.

They told him to stop. BUT HE WOULD NOT STOP!

Finally, he was in so much trouble that he was threatened with death. What would he do?

If he kept on loving these unlovable people, he would be killed.

Only if he stopped loving them could he escape death.

WHAT WOULD *YOU* DO?

Most of us would stop, wouldn't we? But Jesus didn't. Instead, he DIED — because he wanted sinners to know that God would never stop loving them. He even looked down from the cross and said, "Father, forgive them. They don't know what they are doing."

HOW CAN **YOU** BE SURE GOD LOVES YOU even when you do not deserve it? Look at Jesus. There you see God's love in action
  • then and now,
  • for them and for you.

So, Christians consider the death and resurrection of Jesus as EVIDENCE of GOD's GRACE, and in the sacrament of Holy Baptism we ACT OUT the death and resurrection of Jesus in a person's life. Holy baptism is a way of saying,

        "What God did in Jesus, God did for you."
        "Come, receive the gift of grace."

To ACT OUT the death and resurrection we use the **SYMBOL** of water.

When you are UNDER the water, you share in Jesus's death.
When you COME OUT of the water, you share in his resurrection.
And the love of God which we see in the death and resurrection of Jesus
BELONGS TO YOU.

How much water is used or how it is applied makes no difference.
THE DRAMA IS THE SAME.

Some churches completely submerge the person in water. (Immersion)
Others pour water over the person's head. (Pouring)
Others wet the hand and put it on the person's head (Sprinkling)

THE MEANING IS THE SAME. All methods dramatize sharing in the death and resurrection of Christ and receiving God's love as a gift. In the United Methodist Church, all three methods can be used because they all mean the same thing.

But what good does it do to hear God's promise and act it out in a person's life if no one believes it is true? So, the third part of Holy Baptism is **FAITH**. That means trusting God's promise and God's love.

Some churches put so much emphasis on FAITH that they require a person be old enough to make his or her own affirmation of faith before being baptized. They call this "believer's baptism."

Other churches, including The United Methodist Church, put more emphasis on baptism as a GIFT and allow infants to be baptized, *provided* that the parents or sponsors are people of FAITH who receive the gift for the child and PROMISE to teach the child the meaning of baptism. When the child is older and has studied the Christian faith, the child is CONFIRMED. That means the child declares his or her own FAITH in Christ and assumes responsibility for his or her own Christian life. These churches often refer to two kinds of church members — "baptized members" and "confirmed members."

So, the **first** meaning of Holy Baptism is that GOD LOVES YOU and always will love you. God's love belongs to you.

The **second** meaning of Holy Baptism is that YOU BELONG TO GOD. When we share in the death and resurrection of Jesus, we die to the old life of sin which says, "NO!" to God and rise to a new life which says, "Yes!" to God. We don't belong to ourselves anymore. We belong to God, and Jesus is our LORD — our boss.

In many churches, when people are baptized, they are marked with the SIGN OF THE CROSS. They are "branded" with the cross to show that they belong to Christ. All baptized persons are Jesus' disciples, CHRISTIANS who will live under Christ's control and try to be the kind of person he wants us to be.

The **third** meaning of Holy Baptism is that YOU BELONG TO CHRIST'S FAMILY. Hundreds of thousands of people have shared in the death and resurrection of Christ through Holy Baptism. They, too, belong to Christ and we are to live under his control. That makes them all part of

Christ's people, part of Christ's family. We call that family the CHURCH. Through Holy Baptism we are initiated into the Church, and all other baptized Christians become our "cousins" in Christ.

When we talk of the Church in this way, we are NOT talking about a certain congregation that meets in a certain building in a particular town.

We are NOT even talking about a large denomination of Christians such as United Methodist, Presbyterian, Roman Catholic, Baptist, or Assembly of God.

We ARE talking about ALL CHRISTIANS EVERYWHERE. As one hymn says, "All who follow Jesus all around the world! Yes, we're the Church together!"

In some denominations, such as The United Methodist Church, no reference is made to the denomination in the service of Holy Baptism. The only reference is to "Christ's holy Church," which means ALL Christians. That means that you cannot be baptized as a "Methodist" but only as a CHRISTIAN.

Through the centuries, Holy Baptism has become the sacrament for acting out God's grace in a person's life THE FIRST TIME. Since it is possible to do something "the first time" only ONCE, most churches baptize only once. But there is another sacrament which acts out God's grace in our lives over and over again. It is called HOLY COMMUNION.

THE SACRAMENT OF HOLY COMMUNION

This sacrament is known by a variety of names.

Holy Communion	"Communion" is the Latin word for **union with**. In the sacrament we have communion with Christ and communion with other Christians.
The Lord's Supper	We are reminded of the last meal Jesus ate with his disciples the night before he was killed and of Jesus' command to eat this meal in order to remember him.
The Eucharist	"Eucharistia" is the Greek word for **thanksgiving**. In the sacrament, we give thanks to God for the gift of God's grace.
The Mass	Used mostly by Roman Catholics and Anglicans, this name comes from the closing words of the service in Latin "Ite missa est," which means, "Go, you are dismissed."
The Liturgy	Because Holy Communion always has been the most important worship service of the Church, it is THE liturgy of the Church.

The **PROMISE** of Holy Communion is really the same as the promise of Holy Baptism — Christ loves you and always will love you. He loves you so much he would die for you. In fact, he DID die for you.

48

WOULD YOU DIE FOR SOMEONE? Imagine that you see someone in danger. You can save that person's life, but only by losing your own. Would you do it?

If the person were a member of your family, would you do it?
If the person were a close friend, would you do it?
If you don't even know the person, would you do it?
If the person were your enemy, would you do it?

Life is a valuable gift. You must love someone very much to be willing to die for them. JESUS was willing to die so that WE can live, even though we had said, "NO!" to God. That is why we can be SURE of his love. Saint Paul said it in a beautiful way:

> It is not easy to die even for a good [person] — though of course for someone really worthy, a [person] might be prepared to die — but what proves that God loves us is that Christ died for us while we were still sinners."
> — Romans 5:7-8 (TJB)

Holy Communion is another way of sharing in the death and resurrection of Jesus. But the **SYMBOL** is different. In Holy Baptism, we use water. In Holy Communion, we use **bread and wine**. They represent the LIFE of Jesus. During the last meal Jesus ate with his disciples.

> Jesus took a piece of bread, gave a prayer of thanks, broke it, and gave it to his disciples. "Take it," he said, "this is my body."
> Then he took a cup, gave thanks to God, and handed it to them; and they all drank from it. Jesus said, "This is my blood which is poured out for many, my blood which seals God's covenant." — Mark 14:22-24 (GNB/TEV)

You need FLESH if you are to live. Take away too much flesh, and you die. You need BLOOD if you are to live. Lose too much blood, and you die. So flesh and blood make good symbols for LIFE.

> When Jesus said, "This is my body, given for you; this is my blood, given for you," he was saying, "This is my LIFE, given for you."

And whenever we celebrate the sacrament of Holy Communion, we ACT OUT receiving the life of Christ so that we can live.

The bread and wine symbolize Christ's life.
They are given to us.
We eat them.
They become part of us.

Christ's life becomes part of our life. That is UNION WITH. That is "comm-union."

FAITH is part of this sacrament, too. Christ promised to love us, and we trust that promise. Christ promised to be with us whenever his people are gathered together, and we trust that promise. Christ promised that his life, death, and resurrection would give us new life, and we trust that promise, too. Without this faith, the sacrament would be only empty motion. But if you TRUST these promises, the sacrament is a source of strength and life and peace.

You will hear people refer to Holy Communion as a MEMORIAL, a time to remember Jesus. For some people, that is like saying, "Once upon a time, there was this guy Jesus, and this is what happened."

But REMEMBERING is much more important than that!
In a mysterious way, memory brings things back!
The event is RE-CALLED and RE-LIVED.

FOR EXAMPLE:

When you remember a very special party that made you very happy, you not only remember that you were happy at the party, but in your mind the party comes back and you are happy AGAIN.

When you remember something wrong for which you have not been forgiven, in your mind the event comes back and you are ashamed AGAIN.

That's why we like to remember happy times and forget sad ones.

It's that way with Holy Communion, too. The Last Supper looked FORWARD to Jesus giving his life for others. Holy Communion looks BACK to that same death and resurrection.
We re-member it.
We re-call it.
It is there again.
We share in it.
We know God loves us!

Because of this, we can list FOUR important meanings of the sacrament of Holy Communion.

FIRST, we share in the death and resurrection of Jesus, so we can be sure that God loves us even when we do not deserve it, and we can be close to God (comm-union = union with = joined together).

SECOND, we are joined together with (have "union with") all other Christians everywhere.

THIRD, we are thankful for all that God has done. This sacrament is a way of saying, "Thank you, God, for loving us." It is a feast of thanksgiving, a EUCHARIST.

FOURTH, we look forward to fellowship with Jesus in the Kingdom of God at the end of the ages. Christians believe that God wants everyone to live under the control of God's love, and we look forward to the time when everyone will
  • love God,
        • worship God,
              • and obey God
                    "on earth as it is in the heavens."

There are many DIFFERENT WAYS to celebrate Holy Communion. We can
- stand in a circle,
- kneel at a rail,
- sit in the pews,
- use cut bread or broken bread,
  - leavened bread or unleavened bread,
  - white bread or wheat bread,
  - Italian bread or pita bread,
- drink from one cup,
  - drink from separate cups, or
- dip bread into a cup.

However we celebrate, THE MEANING OF THE SACRAMENT IS THE SAME.

HOW OFTEN Holy Communion is celebrated will be decided by church tradition or by the pastor.
- Many churches celebrate the sacrament every Sunday.
- Others celebrate it once a month and on special occasions.
- Some celebrate only four times a year.

And some churches are in the process of changing. For example, in the United Methodist tradition, John Wesley recommended Holy Communion at least once a week, but when the circuit riders were going from town to town that was impossible. So, four times a year became a tradition. Today, many United Methodist churches celebrate Holy Communion the first Sunday of each month and on special festivals, while others share in the sacrament every Sunday.

The frequency of Holy Communion varies widely because
- some people fear that celebrating the sacrament often will cause it to lose its special meaning by becoming too common.
- Others believe that if we know the meaning of the sacrament, frequent celebration will help it gain significance.

HOW DO WE DECIDE? We can start by remembering what Holy Communion means and asking, "How often do we NEED it?"

How often do you need to receive God's love?
How often do you need to be forgiven?
How often do you need new strength and peace?
How often do you need communion with other Christians?
How often do you need to give God thanks?
How often do you need to look forward to the Kingdom of God?

Answer these questions, and you will be able to decide how often you need to celebrate the sacrament of Holy Communion.

HOW MUCH DO YOU REMEMBER?

True or False

    T   F   A sacrament is a special act of worship which acts out God's love.

    T   F   Protestants have seven sacraments.

    T   F   The three parts of a sacrament are: Promise, Symbol, and Faith.

    T   F   Sin means saying, "No!" to God and turning away from God.

    T   F   Grace means "love we earn by being good."

    T   F   Jesus loved only those who loved him.

    T   F   The death and resurrection of Jesus are evidence of God's grace.

    T   F   Holy Baptism is a way of sharing in the death and resurrection of Jesus.

    T   F   The United Methodist Church believes in baptizing infants.

    T   F   One meaning of Holy Baptism is that we belong to Christ.

    T   F   In the United Methodist tradition, you are baptized as a Methodist and become a Christian later.

    T   F   Most churches baptize a person several times.

    T   F   The symbols used for Holy Communion are bread and wine.

    T   F   "Communion" and "eucharist" come from the same language and mean the same thing.

    T   F   The most important thing about Holy Communion is the kind of bread used.

    T   F   Faith is important for Holy Baptism but not for Holy Communion.

    T   F   All Christians should celebrate Holy Communion the same way.

In your own words, write the PROMISE of Holy Baptism.

_____

_____

_____

_____

In your own words, write the PROMISE of Holy Communion.

_____

_____

_____

_____

Tests

What Is An Acolyte? (Test A)

True or False

1.   T   F   An acolyte is any person who follows Christ.

2.   T   F   An acolyte is any person who leads worship.

3.   T   F   An acolyte is a person who follows Christ as Lord and in service to Christ helps the pastor in public worship.

4.   T   F   "Acolyte" comes from a French word meaning "tomato."

5.   T   F   The Greek word *akolouthos* occurs in the New Testament.

6.   T   F   It is more important for an acolyte to help the pastor in worship than to follow Christ.

7.   T   F   All acolytes in all churches do the same things.

8.   T   F   A "duty" is a task required for a certain job.

9.   T   F   "Discipline" and "disciple" come from the root meaning "to teach."

10.   T   F   Acolytes are expected to chew gum in worship.

Choose the proper answer.
1.   *Akolouthos* comes from what language?
      a.   French
      b.   Latin
      c.   Greek

2.   The first responsibility of any acolyte is
      a.   to follow the instructions of the pastor.
      b.   to follow Jesus.
      c.   to help with Holy Communion.

3.   One DUTY of an acolyte is
      a.   to attend acolyte class regularly.
      b.   to brush your teeth after meals.
      c.   to be on time.

4.   One DISCIPLINE of an acolyte is
      a.   to run errands for the pastor.
      b.   to worship regularly, even when not serving.
      c.   to light and extinguish candles.

5.   One Bible verse that uses *akolouthos* talks about
      a.   sheep.
      b.   trains.
      c.   computers.

What Is An Acolyte? (Test B)

1. *Akolouthos* is a Greek word meaning _____.

2. Complete the following sentence: An acolyte is a person

    who (a) _____

    and (b) _____.

3. In the following list of duties and disciplines, make a check mark in front of each DISCIPLINE expected of an acolyte:
    ____ light the altar candles.
    ____ do acolyte assignments on time.
    ____ follow Jesus Christ as ruler of your life.
    ____ help with Holy Communion.
    ____ be courteous and respectful.
    ____ worship regularly even when not serving as an acolyte.
    ____ take care of vestments.
    ____ be faithful in carrying out assignments.
    ____ set a good example for others to follow.

4. List (from memory) five DUTIES of an acolyte in your church.

    a. _____

    b. _____

    c. _____

    d. _____

    e. _____

5. Write (from memory) TWO Bible verses which use *akolouthos*.

    _____

    _____

    _____

    _____

    _____

6. What is the most important thing you have learned about acolytes so far?

    _____

    _____

    _____

The House Of Worship (Test A)

Choose the proper answer.

1. We need to know the "geography" of the house of worship so that we
   a. can show people how smart we are.
   b. know what the pastor is talking about.
   c. don't get lost at church.

2. The NARTHEX is
   a. the entrance way into the church.
   b. the area we sit in for worship.
   c. part of the church kitchen.

3. NAVE comes from the Latin word for
   a. ship.
   b. ox cart.
   c. walking stick.

4. During worship, most of the congregation will sit in
   a. the narthex.
   b. the nave.
   c. the chancel.

5. Worship leaders usually sit in
   a. the narthex.
   b. the altar.
   c. the chancel.

6. SANCTUARY means
   a. a holy place.
   b. a restricted place.
   c. a safe place.

7. The altar or communion table usually is found in the
   a. narthex.
   b. sanctuary.
   c. nave.

8. The focal point of the house of worship is the
   a. altar.
   b. nave.
   c. chancel.

9. The word that means "place of sacrifice" is
   a. alter.
   b. halter.
   c. altar.

10. On a separate sheet of paper, draw a diagram of your house of worship and locate the narthex, nave, chancel, and altar.

The House Of Worship (Test B)

1. The entrance way to the house of worship is called the _____.

2. Worship leaders usually sit in the _____.

3. The congregation sits in the part called the _____.

4. One part of the house of worship has two names. It is called both the _____ and the _____.

5. The word "alter" means _____.

6. The word "altar" means _____.

7. The word "chancel" refers to _____.

8. The word "cancel" means _____.

9. The word "sanctuary" means _____.

10. Must all houses of worship be built the same way? _____

11. Write the Bible verse which talks about fishing.

    _____

    _____

    _____

    _____

    _____

12. Write the Bible verse which talks about light.

    _____

    _____

    _____

    _____

    _____

Christian Symbols (Test A)

True or False

1.   T   F   Symbols are used only in church.

2.   T   F   Symbols can represent something invisible.

3.   T   F   Symbols are the same as pictures.

4.   T   F   Another word for symbol is SIGN.

5.   T   F   Groups of symbols can be read as a story.

6.   T   F   All forms of the cross mean the same thing.

Choose the proper answer.

1.   The fish is an old symbol which means Jesus Christ is
    a. creator.   b. God's son, savior.   c. king.

2.   Three equal circles joined together represent
    a. the Holy Trinity.   b. marriage.   c. a circus.

3.   Alpha/Omega means that Jesus is
    a. alive.   b. creator.   c. beginning and end.

4.   The anchor is a symbol of
    a. hope.   b. love.   c. courage.

5.   Purple represents royalty because it used to be
    a. very pretty.   b. very common.   c. very rare.

6.   The monogram Chi Rho means
    a. Christ.   b. Jesus.   c. God.

7.   The monogram Iota Eta Sigma means
    a. In His Sign.   b. In His Steps.   c. Jesus.

8.   Alpha/Omega, Chi Rho, and Iota Eta Sigma use letters from
    a. Latin.   b. Greek   c. Hebrew.   d. Spanish.

9.   The butterfly is a symbol of
    a. resurrection.   b. eternal life.   c. hope.

10.   A ship represents
    a. the ocean.   b. a vacation.   c. the Church.

11.   Draw your favorite symbol and tell what it represents,

_____

_____

_____

_____

Christian Symbols (Test B)

True or False

1.   T   F   Symbols are the same as pictures.
2.   T   F   Symbols can represent things which are invisible.
3.   T   F   A group of symbols can be read like a story.
4.   T   F   Symbols are used only in religion.
5.   T   F   Symbols help us worship with our eyes.
6.   T   F   Green is a symbol for courage.

Give the **name** and **meaning** of the following symbols.

✝   _____   _____

    _____   _____

    _____   _____

    _____   _____

△   _____   _____

ihs   _____   _____

◯   _____   _____

✡   _____   _____

    _____   _____

    _____   _____

The Christian Year (Test A)

True or False

1. T   F   Calendars and clocks are instruments for measuring time.
2. T   F   Life would be more fun without parties and celebrations.
3. T   F   The Christian Year has always been the same.
4. T   F   The first Christian festival was Easter.
5. T   F   Pentecost means "75 days."
6. T   F   Advent helps us prepare for Christmas.
7. T   F   Epiphany says, "Christ is for everyone."
8. T   F   Easter is always the first Sunday of March.
9. T   F   Lent began as a time to prepare for Holy Baptism.
10. T   F   Lent begins exactly forty days before Easter.

Choose the proper answer.

1. The first SEASON of the Christian year was
    a.   the four Sundays before Christmas.
    b.   the fifty days after Easter.
    c.   the forty days before Easter.

2. The message of Christmas is
    a. "Santa Claus is here."   b. "Look what I got!"   c. "Christ is born!"

3. The word "epiphany" means
    a. "to show forth."   b. "that looks funny."   c. "Jesus is king."

4. The Christian Year
    a.   was developed over a long period of time.
    b.   was created by a special committee.
    c.   is the same for all Christians.

5. The festival which says, "Christ is for everyone" is
    a. Advent.   b. Easter.   c. Epiphany.

6. The festival which says, "Christ is risen!" is
    a. Lent.   b. Easter.   c. Pentecost.

7. Advent is a time
    a.   to prepare for the birth of Christ.
    b.   to celebrate the birth of Christ.
    c.   to finish your Christmas shopping.

8. Christmas begins on December 25 because
    a.   that is the date when Jesus was born.
    b.   all other dates were taken.
    c.   it replaced an old Roman holiday.

The Christian Year (Test B)

On the following chart,
      1. list the seasons of the Christian Year in order.
      2. tell what each season celebrates.
      3. tell when each season begins.
      4. tell what symbolic color is used for the season.

Season	What The Season Celebrates	When It Begins	Symbolic Color

What Worship Is (Test A)

True or False

1.   T   F   Only Christians worship.

2.   T   F   Every person has values to live by.

3.   T   F   Whatever is most important to a person is his/her god.

4.   T   F   What we worship determines the kind of person we become.

5.   T   F   In English, *sebomai* and *proskuneo* are both translated "worship."

Choose the proper answer.

1. Worship is something we
   a   attend.
   b.   watch.
   c.   do.

2. The New Testament words for worship are
   a.   verbs.
   b.   nouns.
   c.   conjunctions.

3. Worship is concerned mainly with
   a.   printed songs and prayers.
   b.   how much God is worth.
   c.   listening to a sermon.

4. Posture refers to
   a.   singing in a loud voice.
   b.   the sanctuary.
   c.   body positions.

5. We act out *sebomai* by
   a. kneeling.   b. standing.   c. sitting.

6. We act out *proskuneo* by
   a. kneeling.   b. standing.   c. sitting.

7. We act out *latreuo* by
   a. kneeling.   b. standing.   c. sitting.

8. Christians worship together because
   a.   they are part of God's family.
   b.   God will hate them if they don't.
   c.   it is the only way to worship.

What Worship Is (Test B)

1. The Anglo-Saxon word *woerthan* meant
    a. "to declare how much something is worth."
    b. "to be."
    c. both of the above.

2. Worship is something we
    a. do.
    b. attend.
    c. watch.

3. As acolytes, we are
    a. helping the pastor put on a show.
    b. helping people worship God.
    c. gaining credits toward heaven.

4. The Greek words translated as "worship" are
    a. nouns.
    b. adjectives.
    c. verbs.

5. The three Greek words which are translated into English as "worship" are

    a. _____

    b. _____

    c. _____

6. _____ means "to lift up" or praise.

7. _____ means "to bow down."

8. _____ means "to serve."

9. Why is it important for Christians to worship together?

    _____

    _____

    _____

    _____

    _____

Ritual And Liturgy (Test A)

True or False

1.   T   F   Ritual is a set way of doing something.

2.   T   F   Rituals allow a number of people to do something together without chaos.

3.   T   F   A liturgy is a special kind of ritual.

4.   T   F   Every liturgy is a ritual.

5.   T   F   Every ritual is a liturgy.

6.   T   F   "Liturgy" comes from a Greek word which means "the work of the people."

7.   T   F   A liturgy is a ritual in which everyone participates.

8.   T   F   A "liturgical church" is one which REQUIRES that a particular liturgy be used.

9.   T   F   The major "liturgical churches" in America are the Roman Catholic, Episcopal, and Lutheran churches.

10.   T   F   A "free church" is one which lets the pastor or congregation determine its own ritual.

11.   T   F   The main "free churches" in America are the Methodist, Presbyterian, and Baptist churches.

12.   T   F   One advantage of a liturgy is that it provides a familiar outline for the worship service.

13.   T   F   A liturgy usually is built around the Christian Year.

14.   T   F   The content of most liturgies comes from the Bible.

15.   T   F   Unless it is used carefully, a liturgy may become rather rigid and mechanical.

16.   T   F   Sometimes liturgies are not changed often enough to keep up to date.

17.   T   F   Not using a set liturgy gives the congregation more voice in determining the order of worship.

18.   T   F   Not using a set liturgy always leads to more creative worship services.

19.   T   F   There is more than one right way to worship God.

20.   T   F   Worship should give us an opportunity to lift up the importance of God, bow down before God, and serve God.

Ritual And Liturgy (Test B)

True or False

1.   T   F   A ritual is a set way of doing something.

2.   T   F   The only place we use rituals is at church.

3.   T   F   Rituals allow people to do things together without chaos.

4.   T   F   A liturgy is a ritual that everyone watches.

5.   T   F   "Liturgy" comes from a Greek word meaning "time to eat."

6.   T   F   A *liturgical* church is one which **requires** that a certain liturgy be used.

7.   T   F   One problem with using the same liturgy all the time is that it can become boring.

8.   T   F   One problem with changing the ritual often is that people do not know what to do.

9.   T   F   The United Methodist Church **recommends** a liturgy but does not **require** that it be used.

10.   T   F   If other Christians do not worship the same way we do, they are not true Christians.

Just For The Fun Of It

Write the Bible verse which uses *akolouthos* and talks about sheep.

_____

_____

_____

Write the seasons of the Christian Year in order and tell what each season celebrates.

_____

_____

_____

_____

_____

_____

_____

The Order Of Worship (Test A)

True or False

1.   T   F   Churches provide an order of worship so that people can know who is putting on the show.

2.   T   F   The order of worship helps people worship together without confusion.

3.   T   F   Every church uses exactly the same acts of worship each Sunday.

4.   T   F   Some denominations print the recommended or required order of worship in the front or back of the Book of Prayer or the hymnal.

5.   T   F   A rubric is a precious gem stone.

6.   T   F   Rubrics are instructions for worship.

7.   T   F   Rubrics are always printed in red.

8.   T   F   Pastors who do not obey all rubrics will be shot at dawn.

9.   T   F   In worship, the greeting is a time to say good morning to everyone.

10.   T   F   A hymn is a poem set to music.

11.   T   F   A prayer which asks God to be present is called an invocation.

12.   T   F   Confession means to admit you have done wrong.

13.   T   F   The Lord's Prayer was made up by a church committee.

14.   T   F   Scripture lessons are usually read from the hymnal.

15.   T   F   The word "creed" comes from a Latin word meaning "true."

16.   T   F   The sermon is the minister's report about church events.

17.   T   F   The benediction says that God wants good things to happen.

18.   T   F   "Amen" is a Greek word which means "stop."

19.   T   F   Jesus was called "the Lamb of God."

20.   T   F   You will be a better acolyte if you know what you are doing.

The Order Of Worship (Test B)

1. The _____ lists the order in which acts of worship are done.

2. Instructions for worship, sometimes printed in red, are called _____.

3. If an order of worship is recommended or required by your denomination, where is it found?

   _____

4. Introductory music which helps prepare for worship is called the _____.

5. A poem of praise set to music is called a _____.

6. A prayer which asks God to be present is an _____.

7. The Lord's Prayer was first taught by _____.

8. "Gloria Patri" is Latin for _____.

9. "Doxology" comes from a Greek word which means _____.

10. A selection of Psalms used in worship is called the _____.

11. The _____ is the part of the Bible which tells how God worked through the lives of the Hebrew people.

12. The word "gospel" means _____.

13. Another word for "epistle" is _____.

14. The _____ is a prayer in which the pastor lifts up the needs of the congregation and the world.

15. A _____ is a spoken message which explains a passage of Scripture and applies it to our daily lives.

16. The _____ is a blessing which says God wants good things to happen to the people.

17. The word "Amen" means _____.

18. "Hallelujah" means "Praise the Lord!" in the _____ language.

19. "Talking to music" is one way to describe a _____.

20. What is the most important thing you have learned about worship?

    _____

    _____

    _____

    _____

The Sacraments (Test A)

True or False

1.   T   F   A sacrament is a way of acting out God's love for us.
2.   T   F   In the Protestant Church, there are only two sacraments — Holy Baptism and Holy Communion.
3.   T   F   The promise of Holy Baptism is that God will love us if we are good.
4.   T   F   In Holy Baptism, water is used to show we need a bath.
5.   T   F   Sin is turning our backs on God and doing what WE want.
6.   T   F   "Communion" is a Greek word meaning "to follow."
7.   T   F   In Holy Communion, the bread and wine represent the life of Jesus.
8.   T   F   "Eucharist" is a Latin word meaning "Christmas."
9.   T   F   The first meaning of Holy Communion is that God loves you.
10. T   F   Jesus told his followers to remember him with bread and wine.

Choose the proper answer.

1. We ACT OUT God's love for us in
   a. the sermon.   b. the Bible.   c. the sacraments.

2. The three parts of a sacrament are
   a.   promise, symbol, and faith.
   b.   faith, hope, and love.
   c.   Tom, Dick, and Harry.

3. The promise of Holy Baptism is that
   a.   God will love you if you are good.
   b.   God will love you all the time.
   c.   God will love you part of the time.

4. Baptized persons are marked with the sign of the cross
   a.   to show they belong to Christ.
   b.   to make them members of The United Methodist Church.
   c.   to give the pastor something to do.

5. "Grace" means
   a. a pretty girl.   b. a free gift.   c. love we earn.

6. In Holy Communion, the bread and wine are
   a. the promise.   b. the symbol.   c. faith.

7. The sacraments are
   a. not important.   b. important.   c. very important.

The Sacraments (Test B)

1. We **read** about God's love in the _____; we **hear** about God's love in the _____; we **act out** God's love in the _____.

2. The three parts of a sacrament are _____, _____, and _____.

3. Protestant Churches recognize two sacraments: _____ and _____.

4. "Sin" means _____.

5. "Grace" means _____.

6. The promise of Holy Baptism is _____.

7. The symbol used in Holy Baptism is _____.

8. In Holy Baptism, going under the water and coming out of the water means _____ _____.

9. The sign of the cross means _____.

10. The promise of Holy Communion is _____.

11. The symbols used in Holy Communion are _____.

12. These symbols represent the _____ of Jesus given to the people.

13. "Communion" means _____.

14. "Eucharist" means _____.

15. What is the most important thing you have learned about the sacraments?

_____
_____
_____
_____
_____

Acolyte Test

(Covering the first four chapters: What Is An Acolyte?, The House Of Worship, Christian Symbols, and The Church Year)

Part I

True or False

1.   T   F   An acolyte is any person who follows Christ.

2.   T   F   Acolyte comes from a Greek word meaning "Christian."

3.   T   F   Helping the pastor in public worship is more important than following Christ.

4.   T   F   Lighting candles in worship is a duty of an acolyte.

5.   T   F   Always being reverent in the house of worship is one discipline expected of an acolyte.

6.   T   F   The entrance to the house of worship is called the nave.

7.   T   F   In most churches, the pulpit is in the chancel.

8.   T   F   "Altar" and "alter" mean the same thing.

9.   T   F   A symbol is a picture of something that cannot be seen.

10.   T   F   Symbols are used only in churches.

11.   T   F   Symbols help us worship by giving us something to see.

12.   T   F   All three forms of the cross (Latin, Greek, Tau) mean the same thing.

13.   T   F   The Christian Year is based on major events in the history of Methodism.

14.   T   F   The coming of the Wise Men is remembered during Epiphany.

15.   T   F   Advent begins four weeks before Christmas.

16.   T   F   Two seasons which use the color white are Epiphany and Lent.

17.   T   F   Lent begins forty days before Easter.

18.   T   F   The season which prepares for the coming of Christ is Advent.

19.   T   F   Pentecost celebrates Christ sending the Holy Spirit on the Church.

20.   T   F   Scripture, prayers, and hymns can express the theme of a season.

Part II

1. List six **duties** of an acolyte.

    _____

    _____

    _____

    _____

    _____

    _____

2. List four **disciplines** of an acolyte.

    _____

    _____

    _____

    _____

3. Write the definition of an acolyte as we have it in our study book.

    _____

    _____

    _____

    _____

4. Write two Bible verses which use *akolouthos*.

    _____

    _____

    _____

    _____

    _____

Part III

Write the meaning of the following symbols

1. _____

2. _____

3. _____

4. _____

5. _____

6. _____

7. _____

Part IV

Choose the proper answer.
1. The Greek word *akolouthos* comes from a verb which means
   a. to worship.
   b. to follow.
   c. to eat.

2. A duty is
   a. something we are required to do.
   b. something we ask to do.
   c. the same as a discipline.

3. A discipline is
   a. a set of rules.
   b. a scolding or spanking.
   c. a habit we form to make our life what we want it to be.

4. An acolyte may be dismissed from service for
   a. being too active in the church.
   b. being unfaithful in his/her service.
   c. being too good an acolyte.

5. Nave comes from a Latin word which means
   a. seat.
   b. ship.
   c. worship.

6. Sanctuary means
   a. a safe place.
   b. a large house.
   c. a church.

7. The Christian Year tells the story of
   a. the life of Jesus.
   b. the history of our country.
   c. how hymns were written.

Part V

List the seasons of the Church Year **in order** and tell what each season celebrates.

_____

_____

_____

_____

_____

_____

_____

Acolyte Test
(Covering all chapters)

1. Acolyte comes from a Greek word meaning _____.

2. An acolyte assists the _____ in public worship.

3. Write two Bible passages which use the word *akolouthos.*

   _____

   _____

   _____

   _____

   _____

4. Write the definition of an acolyte as it is found in the study book.

   _____

   _____

   _____

5. List 4 duties of an acolyte.

   _____

   _____

   _____

   _____

6. List 4 disciplines (life habits) of an acolyte.

   _____

   _____

   _____

   _____

7. The four parts of a house of worship are _____, _____,

   _____, and _____.

8. T   F   "Altar" and "alter" mean the same thing.

9. The word "sanctuary" means _____.

10. Nave comes from a Latin word meaning
    a. ship.
    b. ox cart.
    c. walking stick.

11. The focal point of the house of worship is the
    a. narthex.
    b. sanctuary.
    c. nave.

12. The word which means "place of sacrifice" is
    a. an alter.
    b. a halter.
    c. an altar.

13. T   F   Symbols help us worship by giving us something to see.

14. T   F   Symbols are the same as pictures.

15. T   F   All forms of the cross symbolize God's love.

16. is a symbol for _____.

17. is a symbol for _____.

18. is a symbol for _____.

19. List the seasons of the Christian Year **in order**.

    _____

    _____

    _____

    _____

    _____

    _____

    _____

20. The season which says the Messiah will die for us is called _____.

21. _____ celebrates the fact that Christ is Messiah for everyone.

22. The resurrection of Christ is celebrated during _____.

23. T   F   Advent is intended as a time to celebrate Christmas early.

24. Pentecost celebrates _____.

25. T   F   Lent begins 40 days before Easter.

26. Easter is the first _____ after the first _____ of _____.

27. Christians worship on Sunday because _____.

28. The Christian Year is based on _____.

29. T   F   "Worship" means "to declare how much something is worth."

30. T   F   Worship is a program we attend on Sunday morning.

31. T   F   The New Testament words for "worship" are verbs (action words).

32. *Sebomai* means _____.

33. *Proskuneo* means _____.

34. *Latreuo* means _____.

35. Match the following body postures with what they act out in worship.

standing   confession

kneeling (bowing)   instruction

sitting   praise

36. If a person stops worshiping with the congregation, which of the following problems is likely to develop?
    ____   a. He/she becomes careless about worship.
    ____   b. Private worship becomes incomplete (usually leaving out praise).
    ____   c. Worship is crowded out by other activities.

37. Christians build houses for worship because
    a.   they can't worship without them.
    b.   a special setting helps us worship.
    c.   God will be mad if we don't.

38. A set way of doing something is called a _____.

39. A ritual in which everyone participates is called a _____.

40. T   F   "Liturgy" comes from a Greek word meaning "the word of the people."

41. A church which **requires** a certain liturgy is called a
    a. liturgical church.
    b. free church.
    c. strict church.

42. The United Methodist Church
    a. requires a certain liturgy be used.
    b. recommends a liturgy to be used.
    c. does not provide a liturgy for churches to use.

43. The order in which acts of worship are done is called _____.

44. A poem of praise set to music is called a _____.

45. Admitting we have done wrong is called _____.

46. The _____ is a prayer which asks God to be present.

47. A blessing spoken to the people is called _____.

48. Instructions for worship, sometimes printed in red, are called _____.

49. The two sacraments recognized by Protestant Christians are _____ and

    _____.

50. The sacrament which acts out being buried and raised with Christ is _____.

51. The symbol used in Holy Baptism is _____.

52. The symbols used for Holy Communion are _____ and _____.

53. The sacrament which says we are in union with Christ and other Christians is the sacrament

    of _____.

54. The word "Eucharist" means _____.

55. A special act of worship through which God's love is acted out in a person's life is called a

    _____.

Acolyte Workshop
(Final Test)

1. T   F   An acolyte is a person who follows Jesus Christ as Lord and who, in service to Christ, helps the pastor in public worship.

2. The word "acolyte" means (2 answers)
    a.   to light.
    b.   to follow.
    c.   to help.
    d.   to sing.
    e.   to praise.

3. List two good habits for an acolyte to follow.

    _____

    _____

4. Once an acolyte is chosen, he/she can serve until _____.

5. List three responsibilities of an acolyte.

    _____

    _____

    _____

6. Draw a diagram of our house of worship, labeling each of the following parts: Narthex, Nave, Chancel, and Sanctuary.

7. T   F   "Sanctuary" means "a safe place."

8. When we sing hymns of praise we
    a.   sit.
    b.   kneel.
    c.   lie down.
    d.   stand.

9. T   F   The Altar is always found in the Chancel area.

10. Draw lines to connect the correct phrases

    sebomai   serve (witness)

    latreuo   bow down (pray)

    proskuneo   lift up (praise)

11. As Christians we worship together because we are all part of the Christian _____.

12. T   F   "Amen" is a Hebrew word which means "It is true."

13. T   F   The word "Nave" comes from the Latin word meaning "navy" and is used to describe the section of the church, which, if turned upside down, resembles a ship.

14. It is traditional to talk about three parts of a sacrament. Choose the correct three.
    a.   praise
    b.   promise
    c.   faith
    d.   prayer
    e.   symbol
    f.   water
    g.   wine

15. Another name for the Eucharist is _____.

16. T   F   "Holy Communion" comes from the Latin word meaning "uniform with."

17. T   F   A sacrament is a special act of worship which acts out God's love.

18. The services for the Baptism and Holy Communion can be found
    a.   in the front of our hymnal.
    b.   in the Bible.
    c.   in the back of our hymnal.

19. T   F   It is important how much water is used in Baptism.

20. In Holy Communion, what are the symbols of Christ's blood and body? Choose the correct two.

    a.   wine or juice of the vine

    b.   potatoes

    c.   wheat

    d.   bread

    e.   meat

21. T   F   Grace is the love of God which God gives to us as a gift — we cannot work for it.

22. T   F   A symbol reminds us of something.

23. Draw a line to the correct phrase.

    White   Light; Purity

    Purple   Royalty; Penitence

    Red   Growth

    Green   Blood; Fire; Bravery

24. Draw a symbol which reminds us of the death and resurrection of Jesus.

25. *Leitourgia* is a Greek word for

    a.   lights

    b.   litany

    c.   liturgy

    d.   lamp

26. T   F   All Christians must worship the same way.

27. T   F   The season which prepares us for the coming of Christ is Advent.

28. T   F   A ritual is a set way of doing things.

29. T   F   Easter is always celebrated on the first Sunday after the first full moon after the beginning of spring.

30. T   F   A "Benediction" is a blessing given to the people by the pastor just before the people prepare to leave.

31. Draw lines to the correct phrases.

    Invocation   Psalms used as a congregational response of praise

    Gloria Patri   A short hymn of praise to the Trinity

    Doxology   A prayer which asks God to be present

    Psalter   A short hymn of praise sung when an offering is presented or following a scripture reading

32. T   F   Acolytes should be regular in attendance to worship services even if not acolyting in order to remain familiar with the order of worship and to witness to their commitment to Jesus and the Church.

33. How do you spell Acolyte? _____.

34. T   F   In the United Methodist Church, a person can never be baptized more than once.

35. As part of the responsibilities of an acolyte, he/she shall report to the pastor _____ minutes prior to the beginning of a worship service and _____ minutes prior to a wedding.

Extra Points

Draw a line to the correct season (1 point for each answer).

    Purple   Lent

    White   Epiphany

    Green   Easter

    Purple   Kingdomtide

    White   Advent

    Red   Christmas

    Green   Pentecost